YES DAD, I WANT TO GO TO SEA!

Also by Eric Kemp:

– Captain John Kemp MBE –
A Master Mariner of the 20th Century

'Yes Dad, I Want to Go to Sea!'

Eric Kemp

UNITED WRITERS
Cornwall

UNITED WRITERS PUBLICATIONS LTD
Ailsa, Castle Gate, Penzance, Cornwall.

British Library Cataloguing in Publication Data:
A catalogue record for this book is
available from the British Library.

ISBN 9781852001537

Printed in Great Britain by
United Writers Publications Ltd
Cornwall.

I dedicate this book to

Truro School and HMS *Worcester*,
who trained me very well to face
the life of a mariner;

my wife Jill, and
sons Ian and Jeremy,
who have encouraged me
in the task of writing it.

Preface

My very earliest memories concerning the sea are from recollections of my father who was a master mariner before me. Those first years revolved, in many ways, around his comings and goings. My mother put up with the long lonely days of separation from her husband willingly. She was a fisherman's daughter and well knew the cost of earning a living from the sea. She coped with this difficult wanderlust and managed with a little sick boy wonderfully well. I can only bless her patience and the love which surrounded my early life.

My father was a real live Father Christmas when he arrived home, and I did extremely well from his many presents on these occasions, so this did make a up little for the lengthy absences.

I come from a long line of seafarers. My grandmother was a member of the Hollow family who were ship owners. They originally made their money as captains in the tea clippers running from China and Australia to Great Britain. However, they were very aware of their position in St. Ives society and cut my grandmother off from the family money when she married John Uren, a fisherman.

My great-grandfather, on my father's side of the family, had been a mate in one of the Hollows' sailing ships. Sadly for me, only one grandparent was alive when I came on the scene. Granny Kemp was a member of the Shugg family, who were well-travelled builders and who had spent some time in South Africa at the end of the nineteenth century.

I should have had an elder sister but she died a few hours after her birth in St. Ives, and that will always be a regret to me as an only child. The fact is that my father and mother were so worried about the maternity service in St. Ives in 1937, that they moved to Romford, in Essex, for my birth. Here they felt the hospital facilities were generally much better than in Cornwall at that time.

I suppose it was only natural that I should write the story of my father's life at sea when I retired, as he died just a few months earlier, in 1999. That book was titled: *Captain John Kemp MBE: A Master Mariner of the 20th Century.* Since writing it I have received quite a lot of encouragement to write my own story of life at sea. This book is just a part of that story and I would like to thank my family and those around me, especially my wife Jill who has contributed an immense amount of work to help me in the task, and my sons Ian and Jeremy who have both assisted me. This book is not meant to be just for mariners, and I have tried to keep the language simple and not too technical. I hope you enjoy the read.

Contents

1

Like Father, Like Son

I was an only child, born in Romford, Essex, in June 1937 of Cornish parents; and to those who doubt my Cornish ancestry I would only reply, "If a cat has kittens in the oven they don't come out as pasties!"

I have, in fact, lived all my life in St. Ives since my mother returned in October 1939 at the start of the war. Both my parents came from long established families in my hometown in West Cornwall.

My mother travelled home to St. Ives with me at two years old, together with our black cat 'Buller', arriving at a rented terraced house of 1890 vintage. The property had gas lighting downstairs and only candles to light us to bed at night. In the kitchen we used an ancient Cornish range, known locally as a 'slab', for cooking, which burned your face if you got too close to it, while your back froze in the draught from the cold outside. Bath time found me in a tin tub placed in front of the fire, and I truly say I was never warm in winter and even in summer it was draughty and cold.

One consolation, however, was the position of number 9 Bellair Terrace; as you could look across the wonderful panoramic view of the town, with its granite terraced houses stretching down the Stennack valley, to the blue sea of St. Ives Bay. Across the water, the cliffs and sand dunes on the east side of the bay could be seen. Sitting in my bedroom window I would watch the small coasting ships waiting for a pilot to take them across the bar and into the river, which is the entrance to the port of Hayle, some three miles away.

I do not remember much of the first years of my life and my story really starts in 1941. I was just four years old and sublimely unaware of the desperate battle in which the country was involved to defeat Nazi Germany. My father, a master mariner, was serving as a Royal Naval officer on board HMS *Teviotbank* an ex-merchant ship adapted as a minelayer, working in the North Sea to hinder an invasion of the country. I saw him, on odd occasions, when his ship had been damaged and he would then come home on leave while repairs were carried out at shipyards in the north-east of England.

I have no doubt he was tired and stressed at these times, and that his only child being a headstrong little boy didn't help. I remember one specific occasion that led to a real stand-off. Food was in very short supply and my mother had to struggle very hard to feed us adequately from our meagre rations, so my father could not believe that his young son would not eat beetroot, at any price, and mother's pleading had no effect on me at all.

His face was a study as he watched my mother trying to persuade me to eat some of the vegetable with the small amount of potatoes and meat that was our evening meal. Standing up at the table, and glaring down at me, he ordered my mum upstairs with the words: "Don't worry, Ann, leave it to me, he will eat it today or I will know the reason why!" Then, in a voice that boomed in my ears, I was told to eat the beetroot without delay. That, of course, did not work and just produced tears in plenty, but my mouth remained closed and was not to be opened.

Under the stairs in this house was a cupboard in which our coal supply for household heating was stored, and before long, frustrated by his failure to see the beetroot disappear, he locked me in the coal-hole in the dark. My reaction to this was a much louder volume of crying and shouted demands to be let out from the dark prison. However, on emerging into the light I again refused to eat the beetroot. So it was back into the darkness and more wailing and shouting.

My mother, not used to such scenes and having retired to a bedroom, admitted later in life to covering her ears and trying to ignore the noise coming from the kitchen and below the stairs.

Two hours later my father went upstairs in great frustration and admitted to my mother that he had failed! He later told me that I had won because he was losing precious drinking time at the pub and was unwilling to strike me in any way. So it was my rather shaken mother that let me out of the coal-hole as my father left by way of the front door. I didn't have to eat the beetroot after all! I must admit I still don't eat it to this day.

If *I* was a problem, the cat Buller proved an even greater one to my mother. No other cat in the area was safe from the ferocious animal and, on two occasions that I remember, he was really to distinguish himself. One morning, my mother was most surprised to find our backyard full of feathers. Later, while out with me on a shopping trip, she was informed by a passer-by that she had observed our cat coming out of a nearby garden with a young chicken in his mouth.

"You will have to be more careful, Mrs Kemp," the lady said, "you could be in real trouble if that cat is not restrained."

"Oh dear," replied my mother, "that must have been where all the feathers came from in my backyard."

However, no sign of the chicken itself was ever found.

The second occasion was even more serious. Four doors down the terrace was the home of Mr and Mrs Burrell, and staying with them were no less than eight commandoes training for special war-time missions. These men were given special food rations which included a large portion of steak meat. It was a quiet Sunday morning and Mrs Burrell was on her way to chapel. In the front room her husband was sitting in an easy chair reading the paper. The meat was in the kitchen larder, ready for cooking in the afternoon prior to the return of the soldiers. The good lady looked into the front room before leaving and said, "Now Harry, you watch that dog of ours and make sure he doesn't touch the meat."

"Don't be silly," said Harry. "He is asleep at my feet and not moving, I can assure you."

Mrs Burrell returned some hour and half later and on entering the kitchen found the meat missing from her small larder. Her husband's pleasant little Sunday nap was violently interrupted.

"Harry, the meat is missing!" she shouted as she ran into the front room. "Where is that dog?"

"Here," said Harry, "at my feet. He has not moved since you left."

That did not save the unfortunate man from a real tongue lashing from his wife. Moved to action, he searched the house and the yard before going out into the lane at the back of the house. There he found Buller tucking into the meat in the muddiest part of the lane, making the steak useless. The enraged man threatened to shoot the cat and on this occasion mother was forced to plead for the animal's life.

August 1941 was to be the time that the ambition to go to sea formed in my mind. My uncle, Will Baker, was a privileged man in St. Ives, and his job as head waiter in the Porthminster Hotel entitled him to a telephone. It was about four in the morning when I awoke to the rattle of small stones being thrown against my window. On getting up and poking my head outside, I could just see Uncle Will in the darkness. He asked me to get my mother quickly, and a minute or so later he informed us that father's ship had docked at Falmouth. We were to dress and bring some clothes and could stay in the port while the ship was having repairs.

After a very early breakfast, we made our way to the St. Ives railway station to catch a train. This was very exciting for me as a small boy, because normally I had to stand on the station and wave my father goodbye as the train took him away to sea. Now I was able to watch the small coasters, both in the bay and alongside in Hayle, from the carriage window on the short journey to St. Erth station and the main line.

Then, after an interesting journey to Truro, where we changed trains again, we eventually arrived in Falmouth. As we approached the final station I could see some of the ships in port and I was wildly excited looking for HMS *Teviotbank*.

We were soon settled in at a local hotel on the seafront and I could watch the soldiers manning a large gun outside the hotel, placed there to protect the port. Each day for a week my father

14

would arrive at the hotel and take us down to the docks. Then there was the magical time of climbing the gangway where, at the top, a sailor would salute my father as we came on board. While there, my father would take me up to the bridge where I could observe the dockyard staff and crew working on deck to prepare for a voyage to warmer waters. He would then show me the gleaming brasswork of the ship's steam reciprocating engine from a doorway above the engine room, and the activity in the ship's galley preparing the next meal. I was hooked, and from that very moment I wanted to go to sea when I grew up.

All too soon we were on our way home in the train, and I was not to see my father for a further three long years. Every so often I would receive a letter, together with beautiful drawings of ships and the sea and other interesting scenes; but to all intents and purposes I was an only child of a one parent family.

Sunday was a special day on which my mother would take me to the Primitive Chapel Sunday School building on Bunkers Hill in St. Ives, and then retire home to have a well-earned nap. I took part in my first Sunday School Anniversary at the tender age of three, singing a verse of *All Things Bright and Beautiful*, together with a friend called Raymond Stevens. I can remember the whole congregation having a good laugh, as I demanded, in a loud voice, that Raymond should make some more room on the bench on which we had to stand or I'd fall off!

It seems incredible now, but at the age of four my mother trusted me to walk home alone from Sunday School; that shows how times have changed. So it was, on a sunny day in the summer of 1941, that I had my first black mark.

As an only child with a wanderlust, I would often disappear for long periods of time. Sunday School finished at three o'clock and my teacher, Miss Bessie Ninnis, would solemnly instruct me to go straight home. However, on this particular August Sunday, waiting outside for me to emerge were Dicky Farrell, Leonard Miller and Tommy Prynne, three young boys of five and six who were the leaders of our local gang. As I met them they were wondering what to do to pass the time. All were older than me, and they decided to try and see the ship that was waiting in the bay enter the port of Hayle some four miles from where we were standing in St. Ives harbour. The coaster had a cargo of coal for the power station and was anchored awaiting the pilot from St. Ives before proceeding. I eagerly joined my three older companions as we set off along the western side of St. Ives Bay.

We stopped close to Porthminster Point to admire the four-inch gun covering the bay anchorage, and then walked on a hazardous cliff track to the river estuary of Hayle. By this time the tide had provided enough water for the ship to approach the entrance, and as we sat down at the top of a sand dune the coaster, with streaks of rust disfiguring its grey paint, was making her approach to the shallow water of the sand bar, before entering the narrow channel.

As we watched, we could see three figures on the forecastle standing by a large gun, and that was of great interest to us. Towards the stern we could see the pilot on the bridge talking to the skipper and giving orders to the man on the wheel. While at the stern itself, immediately behind the accommodation, two figures were preparing mooring ropes. Below us the ferryboat man was standing on the bank, also watching the approaching vessel. All too quickly the vessel passed us on the way into the port and we stood up as she passed. Shortly after that the ferryboat man noticed our presence and began running toward us shouting at the top of his voice for us to clear off.

By now the afternoon was nearly over and the chill of evening was approaching. Unbeknown to us, our parents were at home rather worried as to why their offspring had not returned.

As six o'clock approached, many people were setting off to chapel and church for the evening service. Next door to my mother's house, on the right side, lived a life-long Methodist lady called Charity. As she set off for the Wesley Chapel she noticed the harassed look on my mother's face.

"What's the matter, Annie?" she said. "Is there anything wrong?"

"Yes there is," my mother said. "My little boy is missing, he has not come home from Sunday School."

"Really!" said Charity. "I will look out for him on my way to chapel."

At the same time, on the other side of the house, Miss Johnson was leaving to carry out her duties of playing the organ at the local Catholic Church. Her reaction was entirely different.

"I will join you to look for him, and the church congregation will have to sing their hymns without music tonight I'm afraid."

Mother was really grateful, and together with the other parents she began a wide search of the St. Ives area.

Meanwhile, at Lelant, four breathless little boys had stopped running and were considering what to do. Already it was evident that their parents would be cross and they really had to get home as quickly as possible. However, there were the problems of the crumbling cliff path, approaching darkness and the fact that my short legs could not keep me up with the rest. Luckily it was Sunday and there were no trains on the branch line, so the four of us decided the best route home was along the railway track. Here I was at a disadvantage, as I fell over on quite a few of the sleepers and scraped the skin off my knees. My companions took little notice of my complaints, constantly urging me on to a greater pace. I must admit I had a brief moment of triumph when approaching St. Ives station because all three fell over the points and had similar injuries to mine, as well as being covered in grease.

In those days, up to six coaches would be left in the station over the weekend while the steam engine was housed in its own engine shed close to the bridge near the platform. Tired, sore and afraid of retribution, we walked along the platform trying every carriage door to see if we could get inside and hide. None, of course, were open, and so in the end we reluctantly made for home.

Over this time the concern of our parents was nearing panic, and finally they approached the police station for advice. The constable was very helpful and immediately started organising a search, and was even about to call on the help of the commandoes that were then based in the town. Luckily for us he had that native caution of a policeman and asked our anxious parents was anyone waiting at home to see if the kids had come back.

"No," they admitted, "we have been out searching."

"Well," said the constable, "just check, will you, before we start."

All our homes were only a short distance from the police station, so our parents all proceeded home to check.

I had arrived home to find the front door unlocked, but no one in. Scared of what would occur when my mother did arrive back I scuttled up the stairs of our house and got into bed. I then waited in apprehension, and in darkness, to see what the future held. After the longest half hour of my young life, I heard the front door open and my mother's voice calling, "Are you there, Eric?"

"Yes," I answered in a very croaky voice, "I am here."

Mother came pounding up the stairs demanding to be told where I had been. When she saw me she just burst into tears; and held a very frightened little boy in her arms, telling me it was all right as long as I was back unharmed.

One of the other parents sped back to the police station and the search was called off. Meanwhile, I had a good wash and my bruised legs were treated, and I was given a very welcome hot drink in front of the kitchen slab before being put to bed.

Next morning came the reckoning; my mother imposed a strict curfew and I was only let out in her company for the next fortnight. There was no playing with the gang, and I was accompanied to and from Sunday School. Also, to make matters worse, all the adults we met in town wanted me to tell them what I had been doing to deserve such a punishment. Dicky, Leonard and Tommy suffered a month of similar treatment as well as a real tongue lashing and a clip across the ear.

I must say as I remember these events, that today they would seem impossible, given the worry about the safety of children. In my childhood, such adventures led me to a life at sea, and I am sure they made up a part of my character which set me in good stead in later life.

Late in August 1942, on a bright sunny day, I had accompanied my mother to Porthmeor Beach on the northern side of St. Ives, and overlooked today by the New Tate Gallery. In those days a gasworks stood on the gallery site and we were below it on the western end of the beach. I was busy in the early afternoon

18

catching crabs and small fish in a rock pool some fifty yards away from where my mother was sitting on the sand. Close to her was a lady knitting a garment of some kind. Suddenly two planes appeared, diving in from the east above the gasworks. One dropped a bomb right into the large gas holder and an explosion and fire followed. The other dropped a bomb on a house on the hill above the beach, killing its only occupant. The first aircraft fired its machine guns, strafing the sand as people ducked behind rocks or any other shelter available. I simply stared at my mother who was shouting at me to stay were I was, which I did. I can remember the whine of the bullets and seeing the ladies knitting reduced to small pieces of wool. Amazingly no one on the beach was hurt and, shortly afterwards, we were directed away to the far westerly side of the beach where we climbed the cliff to make our way home.

On our return we discovered that Bellair Terrace had many broken windows, but we were lucky and our house escaped without blast damage. Staying with us at the time was an evacuee called Gerald (one of three that stayed with us during the early years of the war) and to my mother's alarm he was missing when we arrived home. It turned out that he had volunteered to help fight the fire at the gasworks and came home later that evening with a blackened face and very dirty clothes, but a bit of a hero really.

One more event during the war was to affect me in later years and help on my path to becoming a Christian. During the whole of 1944 our doctor made many attempts to get me into the local hospital to have a tonsil operation. Time after time I would be sick with an extremely infected throat and the operation would have to be postponed. As a result I did not attend school at all for the whole year.

Then, early in 1945, the doctor called and asked my mother, "Is your son well this morning, Mrs Kemp?"

As luck would have it I had recovered from the latest bout of trouble, and before I knew what was happening, I was in the doctor's car and on my way to the hospital in Hayle for the operation.

That evening I was operated on and all, apparently, went well at the time. However, the next morning I awoke feeling sick and I called the nurse who brought a bed pan. To her horror it filled with blood, and my life was in immediate danger. I can remember the screens being put around the bed and some half dozen or so sisters dressed in black praying around me.

It turned out that the doctor could not be contacted and it fell to the senior sister, Therese, dressed in white, to stem the flow of blood in my throat.

Those prayers were answered, even though I cried and yelled through most of the treatment and that can not have helped. Certainly I owe my life to those prayers and that wonderful Sister Therese. Of course, I realise now, in retrospect, just how difficult I must have been.

I remained in hospital for a fortnight, and for twelve days would eat nothing more than eggs. Needless to say, they were in short supply and I managed to eat all that the hospital had and most of the rations from my mother and her five sisters. At the end I was refused any eggs over the last two days and did eat some bacon. I am sure they were glad to see the back of me when I finally left to return home.

2

Growing Up

In 1946, when I went back to school, I was a whole year behind my class mates, and indeed I only slowly made up that lost time in scholastic ability. Even when I came to take the 11-plus exam I failed to reach grammar school entry standards, and it was only after a year in the St. Ives secondary modern school that, with my parents encouragement, I was able to get a place at Truro School (a Methodist public school). So it was that I started a whole new chapter in my life. As a boarder I was now away from home and the influence of that school has been with me ever since.

It was certainly daunting to be shown into the majestic main building of Truro School, which was already a famous landmark in Cornwall. I can remember prefects staring down at me and filling me with dread as I prepared to see my mother disappearing down the drive of the school, and realised that I was on my own for the first time in my short life.

My immediate experience was salutary, to say the least, as I joined a queue of boys entering the dining room for my first meal away from home. I had been a very finicky eater at home and my mother would always have trouble getting me to eat most foods. Now, as I sat down at a communal table, I looked with horror at a small fishcake placed in front of me. Using my knife and fork I pushed it around the plate with no enthusiasm to eat it at all. The boy next to me on the table had been at the school for a year.

"Don't you like fishcakes?" he said, with his mouth full.

"No," I said, "I don't."

"Never mind," he said, "I'll eat it for you."

The offending fishcake disappeared as if by magic.

"What's next?" I enquired of my so-called new friend.

"Nothing mate. You will only have two pieces of bread and butter with your tea."

It didn't take long at school for me to become as hungry as the rest. Indeed my food disappeared just as fast as everyone else's, and with the help of sport and exercise I soon began to grow quite quickly.

My first year was not really happy. I must admit I was bullied at times and did not get on all that well with my fellow scholars. It all came to a head at the beginning of my second year. A boy in our class had a penknife with blue panels on the side and I also had one which was exactly the same. One day he lost his and accused me of taking it, and I had a rough time from the rest of the class as they believed him.

So I became an outcast because I refused to give up my penknife. By the second day, I had had enough of the bad treatment and resolved to run away. Following our 8pm evening study at prep I slipped out of the class and, instead of returning to my dormitory, I set off down the lane to return home to my mother.

After walking through the city and onto the road leading west I decided that a ride was better than walking. Resolving not to tell any lies I thumbed a lift from the passing cars. Before too long a farmer picked me up and asked me:

"Where are you going, boy?"

"Home to St. Ives," I truthfully replied, and to my intense relief the good man did not ask any more questions. In fact he dropped me off some nine miles further on. Here I waited at a bus stop and used sixpence out of my meagre amount of money to get to Camborne, where I spent the rest of my money on a cup of tea and a bun at a late night café.

Then I was back out on the road, and surely luck was with me because some five hundred yards down the road another car stopped to pick me up. This driver was a very different proposition to the first. Following news of my destination he wanted to know what school I attended.

"Truro School," I replied.

"Boarder or day boy?" he continued.

Now the truth was catching up on me. "Boarder," I replied slowly.

"Well, what are you doing here at this time of night?" was the next question.

I could only answer, "I have run away."

On went the brakes and the gentleman turned the car around. "Now, my boy, you are going back to face the music. As a matter of fact, I went to school with your headmaster Mr Creed."

My heart sank as the car rapidly returned to Truro School and the meeting with the headmaster.

On entering Mr Creed's study I waited miserably while the two men exchanged greetings. What, I wondered, was the punishment going to be?

To my surprise the tone of the interview was very mild. It seemed they had prefects out all over Truro looking for me and the police had also started a search. However, after questions to my class mates, the tale of the knife came to light and the fact that the other boy had found his on returning to his bedside locker. I faced a night in sickbay and then back to school next day, where to my surprise, I found I had some new friends all wanting to know what had happened and eager to tell me of the uproar my absence had caused.

From then on the bullying diminished and I began to have a far happier time at school. Even so, I was not good at my school subjects. Sport dominated my life and my thoughts were turning to my ambition to go to sea, as my father had done before me.

My mother was the first to realise that I wanted to go to sea. She saw that I enjoyed various trips on ships with my father after he had left the Royal Navy and returned to the Merchant Navy.

Shortly after the end of the war I was to have a voyage on the SS *Rowanbank*, 7262 gross tons. This ship was an American Liberty vessel, built during the war as the SS *Samford*, and was my father's first command in 1947. We sailed from Liverpool to Tynemouth and I had a wonderful time on board, even having a steering lesson from the second officer during his watch while we were approaching the north-eastern tip of Scotland, off Fraserburgh. Eventually I was to serve in three vessels of this class later in my own career at sea.

As sailors say, my mother could see the way the wind was blowing, and I don't think at that stage she was keen for me to earn a living at sea. So, at the tender age of twelve, she set me a test. Being a St. Ives fisherman's daughter her contacts in the fishing fleet at St. Ives were many and she arranged for me to have a trip in a local fishing boat called the *Sweet Promise*. This boat was approximately forty feet long and was fishing some forty miles north-west of St. Ives. On the deck, when putting to sea, she carried thirty-six baskets containing lines with five thousand two hundred hooks to catch fish deep down near the sea bottom. The boat was usually at sea for a couple of days and was, in fact, a stern test of my determination to be a sailor.

All went well at first, when we reached the grounds and set the lines and waited for twelve hours before hauling them in. That evening I helped with the work on deck, but just before midnight the skipper, Mr Ernie Stevens, advised me to turn in below as a spell of bad weather was on the way. I obeyed, and by morning things had changed completely. The fishing had not been good and the *Sweet Promise* now faced a bumpy trip back to St. Ives with a westerly gale on her beam and the smell of the diesel engine filling the accommodation and wheelhouse.

Yes, I was soon seasick and it was a miserable time, but it passed when the boat returned to port. My mother nearly disowned me when she heard that my determination to go to sea remained intact.

In all my days at sea I have only been sick a further three times. Once on another fishing boat called *Our John* from St. Ives, then on being an officer in the Trinity House Steam Vessel Service, when I spent three hours repairing damage to a buoy marking a shoal of rocks just outside St. Ives Bay in very heavy swell conditions, and lastly on the Isles of Scilly ferry *Gry Maritha,* in

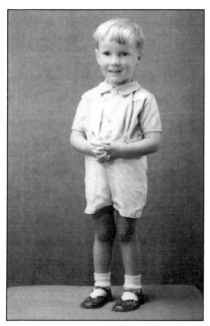

Eric at four years old.

Eric with his mother and father, 1941.

Eric centre front with friends.

The Gang, 1948.

St. Ives Primary School – Class 3A, 1946.

Eric at 12 years old, going to Truro School.

HMS *Teviotbank* – Eric visited his father on this ship as a boy.

Entrance to Hayle harbour.

Truro School main building, 1953.

Truro School Scout Group – Eric fourth from left on back row.

Fore Street Methodist Chapel Sunday School, August 1952.
Eric on the right carrying the banner.

SS *Rowanbank* – Eric had an early voyage on this
ship with his father Captain John Kemp MBE.

a severe north-west gale crossing to the islands. Each time, you may notice, in Cornish waters despite having travelled right around the world in other waters, sometimes in very severe weather!

A year after I had run away from school, my father arrived home. He was now an experienced captain in the Merchant Navy. He quite naturally asked me what I wanted to do with my life and it was then that I informed him of my desire to make my living at sea.

He really did try to change my mind, but stories of poor food, grumpy captains, poor weather and not a great deal of home life failed to persuade me, and eventually he agreed.

He then made an offer for which I was very grateful. He would pay for me to attend the HMS *Worcester*, a training ship moored at Greenhithe on the Thames, provided that I promised to stay at sea until I had qualified to be a master mariner. I agreed to the bargain, and so my life at sea was to begin.

My interview to be a cadet in this very propitious training establishment was quite an eye-opener. My mother and I had travelled to Greenhithe (a small riverside port on the Thames between Dartford and Gravesend) by train, then a taxi carried us to the wooden landing jetty. Before me the ship loomed large, with its black and white painted sides and tall masts reaching to the leaden sky above. Alongside this massive training vessel was the famous sailing ship the *Cutty Sark*, both vessels were moored by massive chains running down into the muddy dark brown river. Downriver I could see a large paper mill at Swanscombe with a small ship discharging wood pulp at the riverside jetty. Looking upriver the jetties and mooring buoys of Greenhithe were all busy with large numbers of coasting vessels owned by the Everard shipping company. Scattered around the horizon, on both sides of the river, were the gigantic chimneys of a power station and numerous cement factories. Everything on the landing jetty, not covered by the rising and falling river level, was coated in cement dust. Out in the river there seemed to be a never ending line of ships, both large and small, passing by and gripping my attention as we waited for a boat to transport us out to this strange and exciting new world.

25

Before long a smart gig with a crew of a coxswain (a cadet captain, no less) and four cadet oarsman came to collect us. I was to learn that this was the second gig, reserved for officers and visitors. The captain's first gig was an even smarter craft, while the jolly boat, which was used for routine movement of cadets etc., was a really basic working boat.

The interview took place after we had been shown around the ship. Below the upper deck of the vessel were the captain's and officers' cabins set towards the stern of the ship, while forward was a cleared space for assemblies and a mess room for meals, together with a galley and rather basic washrooms and conveniences. Also a room which all new cadets came to fear; namely the Cadet Captain's cabin. Here each night cadets would muster to find out who had fallen foul of the many rules on board. Most of my appearances there were because I did not press my trousers properly, or my belt had not been cleaned, or my shirt changed. Punishment was dished out by the Chief Cadet Captain and consisted of extra work in our own time or a beating with a long bamboo cane which really stung. Below this deck were two living decks with chests placed in neat lines to contain our uniforms and necessary work and sports clothes. This was the only space that we could call our own but was, of course, open to inspection at any time, and became another cause for a beating if it was not tidy and shipshape. Above our heads long frames were hinged to the deck head. These were lowered in the evening and we then slung our hammocks on them to sleep in rows above our chests.

Below was a deck where we went to our classrooms and there were various other stores, while the lowest deck had a few secret spaces to have a crafty cigarette and risk a beating if we were caught. Up on the top deck we would walk around in the evening in an event called slewing. About ten of us hailed from Cornwall and we would link arms and walk around the main deckhouse discussing many worldy subjects.

Returning to that first day and my interview. It all seemed a blur to me and I must admit I was apprehensive as I was shown into the august company of Captain Steels VC, the ship's commander. With him were the headmaster, ship's chaplain and chief officer.

They asked me about my school, and seemed impressed with my mother's description of my father's position in the Andrew Weir Company and the fact that the majority of his voyages were of two years length. Anyway, all was well and I was to start in January 1953.

I must say that I went back to Truro School that summer with a spring in my step. I was going to sea, and it was all I could do to wait for the end of the next term and be on my way at last. However, there was one last incident before I left the school with which I would leave my mark.

The main school was designed like an E with the front of the building (the back of the E) facing down over the city of Truro. A really splendid vista, with the tall cathedral towering above the buildings and the whole city visible from the school in those days. At the very front of the building, enjoying this view to its best advantage, was the sickbay. Running back from this section of the building were two large additions containing two dormitories each. Above the upper dormitory was common roof space connected to the front section of the building where the sickbay was located. The sickbay had two large ventilation spaces in the ceiling covered with a gauze to allow a good circulation of air to the room below.

Right under one of these ventilation shafts was a boy who always seemed to be sick. He was small and timid, and his thick rimmed glasses made him a good target for a joke. So one of my close friends paid him a visit on a Saturday afternoon and told him extensive tales about Dracula, ending with the thought that several boys had seen him at the school over past years.

On the next afternoon, I was helped to get up into the roof space through a trapdoor in our washrooms at the far end of the building from the sickbay. I then gingerly made my way across this space until I was right above his bed and could observe him from above. He had his tea on a tray and was eating away peacefully when I hissed in a threatening voice: "Dracula has come to get you!"

27

Up went the tray in the air, drenching the bed clothes with jam and milk, as the boy disappeared under the sheets.

I took off in a bit of a panic, as I had not meant to have such a dramatic effect and could have been caught in the act. As it was, in my haste my foot slipped on one of the rafters and landed on the ceiling of the first dormitory, leaving a long crack for all to see. To say I was relieved to be helped down in the washroom and not be discovered was an understatement.

Next day there was an investigation under way but my friend and I kept very quiet and got away with it.

3

A Cadet on HMS *Worcester*

Now a new life was to begin, and in my first term I was to find that going to sea was not as glamorous as I had thought.

To begin with, it was quite an art to get the hammock properly adjusted and, like many others on the first night, I fell out as the wretched thing turned upside down when I tried to get in. Fortunately a fellow cadet in my division soon showed me the proper way to adjust it and climb in, and I must say that I generally slept well while undergoing training. Just the same, life on the ship was exhausting.

One was awoken at five minutes to seven in the morning to the sound of the bugle playing reveille and you had just three minutes to be out of your hammock, urged on by a cadet captain, or a senior badge cadet, who would simply turn the hammock upside down if you ignored his demands. By quarter past seven your hammock had to be taken down and stored neatly in the space allowed on each sleeping deck, and you were up and dressed in sports gear for a half hour of physical training on the upper deck whatever the weather. Then you had fifteen minutes to put on your working uniform and get up to the dining room for your spartan breakfast.

Forty-five minutes later we were mustered at divisions, where our cadet captain in charge would inspect the state of our uniforms for which I would quite often be in trouble. Then it was on to a normal working day, with lessons and short breaks until four in the afternoon when we had free time for an hour to shine shoes, press uniforms, get our dirty clothes to the laundry and so on. Following the evening meal we had an hour's personal study, then a mug of thick cocoa and half an hour walking around the upper deck before we retired to the sleeping decks. Once more we would line up and get our hammocks out, and an exhausting day would come to its natural end with the playing of lights out by bugle call.

On Wednesdays we had a half-day break from lessons, while on Saturday's we all suffered the process of cleaning the ship in the morning, then on both these days we had sports and free time in the afternoons.

Saturday morning was a bad time for all junior cadets. Under the control of senior badge cadets (the first sight of rank and one which I never achieved) we were lined up on the accommodation decks and given a broom, then we scrubbed the wooden planks in formation, with the constant urging of those in control, for over two hours with short breaks every half an hour. It hardened your hands with blisters and strengthened your back and limbs, scrubbing away accompanied with shouts of "Stop! Turn around and scrub back!" echoing around the vessel. Outside decks were hosed down and the more senior amongst us did those jobs. On more than one occasion during this time I found myself in trouble for breaking one of the many rules that governed our life. Normally this meant that you got a beating from the senior cadet captain. However, if you were late to a muster or slacking at work, you could be sentenced to several hours of extra work on your half days off.

On one such occasion, a group of ten or so of us were sent to scrub the upper deck on a Sunday morning after our normal Sunday service. Normally we had one service a month, when we marched to the Parish Church in Greenhithe. On the other Sundays we had a service on board and then had the rest of the day off. On this day I was not happy at the punishment for some reason, and I soon found myself expressing the view that we should not have extra work on a Sunday as it was a day of rest!

This proved a very popular view amongst our work party, so when the cadet captain went below to the toilet we held a council of war and decided to down tools as it was a Sunday.

On his return the cadet captain found us sitting cross-legged on the deck refusing to work. Threats of a beating had no effect, and before long Chief Officer Mr Donner arrived and demanded we start work, but his orders had no effect either.

So it was that Captain Steele VC arrived on the upper deck in a furious temper. In his experience he had never heard of a mutiny on the *Worcester* and in a voice like thunder he ordered us to work or we would be expelled from the ship forthwith. He wanted to know who started all this and I was pushed forward as the ring leader.

"Well, Cadet Kemp, I am waiting for an explanation for your behaviour," he demanded.

Standing to attention I spoke up, "Sir, I do not believe in extra work on a Sunday. And, additionally, as a Methodist I am not allowed to go to my own church while serving on this ship."

At first words almost failed our famous Captain Steele, then he said, "Very well, get back to your work and I will consider your complaint."

This had the right effect and rather like sheep we went back to work. Some twenty minutes later the cadet captain received orders to release us on Captain Steele's orders. Following that I was never again forced to do extra work on a Sunday.

After a couple of terms on the ship you learned the way out of the torture of cleaning and scrubbing, and I was no exception to that rule. The work boat of the ship was the jolly boat which had a duty crew from each of the different divisions of cadets. These crews, while on duty, were excused the normal day's work-load such as the routine cleaning. At night, however, the jolly boat became the tier boat, and a special crew, along with the first and second gigs' crews, slept on a clear space close to the cadet captain's cabin. This crew made any night trips needed and on Saturdays they covered the day trips and were allowed to work on the boat's maintenance, which was a lot easier than toiling in the general cleaning regime. I was to spend a lot of time in all these boats.

For one term I had the job as a worker on the famous *Cutty Sark* and became familiar with the accommodation while keeping it in as ship-shape condition as possible. Sadly this beautiful sailing ship had all her top sail masts cut down at this time and the college did not have the money to look after her properly. However, it was an education to explore the crew spaces. On the main deck were fifteen sleeping berths shared by thirty sailors. Fifteen turned out on watch as fifteen came off duty to take their places. In the bow compartment was a crude wooden stocks with the chains still in place to hold defaulters.

Our duties were to polish the main furniture in the officer and passenger accommodation towards the stern and keep it as clean as possible, as well as wash down the decks and move the cement dust which covered everything. The cargo holds contained sand ballast and were generally left alone, only being checked occasionally for leaks or other problems.

One thing did amaze me, and that was the condition of the hull on this beautiful tea clipper – it was sheathed in copper and in really good condition, even after all the years of sitting in the Thames off Greenhithe.

It was a sad time when, on a foggy day in 1954, the Duke of Edinburgh visited the *Worcester* to take over the *Cutty Sark* on behalf of a trust. He inspected all of us ranged on deck in our best uniforms and then gave us a pep talk on the importance of the Merchant Navy to our nation.

In actual fact I nearly missed the inspection by the Duke on this occasion. All the cadets were in position on the upper deck and waiting some thirty minutes before the event started. As a member of the second gig crew at the time, I was on stand-by to man the boat for guests should it be needed. Meanwhile, the order was passed that no one was to join the massed ranks late.

Of course, typically, I was summoned out of the ranks to man the gig some twenty minutes before the inspection was due to start, and I was then ordered by our senior cadet captain not to return.

However, determined not to miss the event, I joined the ranks some ten minutes later in a somewhat breathless condition. My division cadet captain was furious, and inspected me again, jamming my cap well forward on my head and making me look rather silly, but other than this I got away with it as there were no further reprisals.

Later we manned the ship's starboard side to give our final salute to the departing *Cutty Sark* as two powerful river tugs waited for the final mooring chain to be cut and then began gently towing her away into the fog bank. In the end it was the *Cutty Sark* which was to have the last word on leaving her riverside moorings. As she came clear she responded to the forward movement of the tug like a racehorse at the off and surged ahead, almost over-running the tug. It was quite a little time before the two tugs regained control and the grand ship disappeared upriver in the gloom, bound for Greenwich.

On two occasions I experienced a welcome break from the routine of the ship. At the end of the summer term of both years on the training ship I was allowed to seek a voyage in one of Everard's coasting vessels before going home on holiday. In the first year I travelled to Goole in Yorkshire and with one companion, Archie Cram, obtained a trip from there to Plymouth in one of the best Everard vessels: the MV *Singularity*. This fifteen hundred ton coaster had previously been painted completely white and had been a participant in the Spithead review carried out by the Queen. Now she had returned to her normal colour of yellow. Her captain was named Roberts and like the chief officer he was from North Wales. The second officer was Irish and complained regularly because the captain and chief officer conversed in Welsh which he could not understand.

Our coastal voyage was enlivened by the fact that a sister vessel, the MV *Similarity*, was a bare three miles ahead of us leaving the Humber, and as she was bound for Newhaven much of our route was the same. The race was on, but despite the best efforts of the engineers and the captain our ship was unable to catch her before she arrived at her destination.

On approaching Start Point, near Plymouth, we were confronted with a navigation problem, the Royal Navy were holding a major exercise and ships like ours were ordered to avoid the area. This meant that we would arrive at 5am on a Sunday morning at our destination, instead of midnight on the Saturday. In that case the company would have had to pay the crew a half day's extra pay for a Sunday at sea. Our captain was quite unwilling to authorise such a payment and just sailed straight through the area. A naval patrol vessel soon challenged him by signal lamp to identify his ship. After ignoring the request for nearly half an hour he eventually sent a message saying he didn't understand, and by the time the navy reacted we were through the prohibited area. Indeed, we did arrive at midnight and the crew did not get their extra money.

My second voyage with the company found myself and two companions joining the MV *Superiority*, a larger vessel of 2600 gross tons. We joined her at a wharf near Greenhithe where she was loading a cargo of cement in bags for Plymouth. This vessel was a very different proposition to the *Singularity*. Her captain had been a deep sea man and was not used to coasting vessels. She carried three deck officers and the chief mate soon made it very clear that he expected us to work our passage on the ship. We were to sail for three weeks and we had to pay six shillings a day for our food.

Fortunately the ship had been unable to get an engineers' steward, so we agreed to share his duties and share his pay equally amongst us. The work included fetching food from the galley and serving it to the engineers in their mess room, washing the plates and cups in a very small washroom, keeping the mess itself clean and helping the cook in the galley when required. On the other two days the chief gave us deck jobs like painting, chipping and washing down. I must admit we didn't work too hard at these tasks as we were paying for our food and felt a little aggrieved that there was no payment for this extra duty.

The fun really started when we reached Plymouth. Everard ships were known for not taking pilots to guide them into ports where it was not compulsory, and at Plymouth that was the case for the *Superiority*. Nonetheless, the captain was nervous and so hoisted the G flag of international signals, meaning I require a pilot at the entrance to the port. Nothing happened for two hours and then a local pilot boarded with a cheerfully smiling face and apologised to the captain:

"Sorry," he said, "no one ashore could believe that an Everard vessel would need a pilot so nobody checked his flag signal."

Our captain was not amused and became even less so when, under the pilot's guidance, we crashed into the quayside. The ship was then delayed for a couple of days whilst repairs took place to the ship and jetty. When the captain went to the agent's office in Plymouth, the company superintendent made his displeasure known at this outcome and the captain was ordered to leave without a pilot or change his employment.

While in Plymouth the crew engaged in a lot of heavy drinking at the pubs. I had taken the chance to return to St. Ives and get some fresh clothes and ask mother to wash my dirty gear.

On the first night after returning I was startled to see the cook, well under the influence of alcohol, *frying* a cooked pasty and announcing to all who would listen that it was a wonderful tasty meal. My only comment was not voiced, but my thought was: 'I rather you than me!'

After a week's stay we left the jetty with a rather tricky south westerly wind blowing and without the help of a pilot. As a result we managed to get entangled in the moorings of a number of yachts, damaging two of them, and by the time we had arrived outside the Plymouth breakwater the captain was a very worried and irritable man. We then proceeded to Emden, in the British Zone of Germany, to load a cargo of coal for the port of Aalborg in Denmark.

There followed a very pleasant stay in which we visited the various lakes around the town of Aalborg with the aid of the ship's motor lifeboat. We also enjoyed the many entertainment parks and restaurants during our stay.

However, a problem was about to leave me in a certain amount of trouble. While I was working on deck during the stay a small piece of coal grit got into my eye. I had to attend a hospital as the grit scratched my eyeball and was most painful and this visit cost me most of my money, leaving me wondering how I would get home at the end of the voyage. My companions were by now suffering likewise as they had also spent most of their money in this lovely friendly port.

So it was that we left Aalborg bound for Blyth, from where we were due to return home. As soon as we reached the North Sea we ran into a north-west gale and the *Superiority*, with her slow speed of only eight knots, performed all the mad gyrations that a coaster without any cargo in her holds could.

As luck would have it, on my day as steward the engine broke down and left the ship wallowing in the sea without power. All four engineers were working flat out to get the engine going again and did so after five hours of toil. On this occasion both of my companions were seasick but after my experiences in the St. Ives fishing boat I survived the ordeal. Later I wished I had been sick because the engineers appeared for their food covered in grime and oil and spread it all over the mess room. That proved a hard day, but even with the overtime earned, I still only had ten shillings when we left the ship in Blyth once I had paid my food bill, and my companions were in the same situation.

We were able to find enough money between us to get to Newcastle Central Station where we presented ourselves to a surprised ticket clerk. "We have not got enough money to get home and could you help?" we asked.

"Well lads," he replied, "have you got enough money to ring home and get the money paid by telegraph?" We all agreed we would try.

My companions came from Helston in Cornwall and Poole in Dorset and they were able to get through to their parents right away, but my mother was on an outing and did not arrive home until late evening, by which time I had returned to the station with the sad news that I could not provide the money needed to travel.

The clerk luckily took pity on me and issued an IOU to British Railways for four pounds nineteen shillings and sixpence. He took my mother's phone number and promised to phone before he left work at midnight.

Meanwhile I was on the train to London and having to explain to every ticket inspector between Newcastle and St. Ives why I did not have a ticket. Fortunately all was well on my arrival home as my mother paid the money into the local station at St. Ives.

My last term on the *Worcester* found me in the ideal job – I was appointed boathouse hand. So on Saturday mornings I would come ashore from the ship and look after and clean the two racing gigs housed in the boathouse by the landing stage. Here I would keep all in order; but in truth there was little to do. The ship's gigs were kept in immaculate condition and I spent much of my time in the village café chatting to some of the local girls and dodging anyone in authority who happened to come ashore during the morning.

In other ways, though, there was some strain by the end of 1954. I had been on the *Worcester* two years and this was the minimum you could spend on the ship before leaving for an apprenticeship at sea. To do so you had to attain a leaving certificate and I found I had to work hard even to get the lowest certificate granted.

There was one part of being on this wonderful training ship that really suited me, and that was to observe the never ending traffic of merchant vessels passing up and down the river. All the ships of the famous British shipping lines visited the river at some stage, and I never tired of watching them with their company colours, often dipping their ensigns in salute to HMS *Worcester*.

4

Apprenticeship

Over the two years training I had watched many ships, but it was the beautiful colours of the Ellerman Lines which really caught my eye and inspired me to try and join them.

Amongst the ships regularly passing us were the four passenger ships carrying up to 108 passengers and making regular twelve week round voyages to South Africa from London's West India Docks. These graceful and impressive vessels regularly caused many of us on board *Worcester* to stop and watch as they passed. One could often see some of the brick red antifouling paint showing above the waterline where it met the light grey of the ship's hull. Above that, at the main deck level, a large white band of paint joining the white painted accommodation gave an impression of grace, speed and a wonderful design; and when put together with the buff coloured masts and cargo derricks and the really distinctive buff, white and black funnel I was really captivated. Of course, we also saw, from time to time, the various cargo vessels of the company, and even if some were elderly they also all looked attractive. It was therefore these larger vessels that caught my imagination. The company ships were running to most parts of the globe except South America and they were all named by the prefix '*City of*' (*Port Elizabeth*, *London*, *Calcutta* and so on).

So it was in late November 1954, together with three other

cadets, I presented myself, suitably clothed in my best cadet's uniform, at the office of the Ellerman & Bucknall Steamship Company, 104 Leadenhall Street, London EC3. In my possession was my very precious ordinary leaving certificate from HMS *Worcester* as well as my school reports. Neither were brilliant by any standard but I had just obtained the sixty percent mark in Navigation, Mathematics, Physics, English Language, Literature, Geography, French and History, and last but not least, Seamanship. This was the minimum standard required to get a job in a company such as Ellerman's and to my delight I had acquired it in the minimum time to pass through the training system.

This now entitled me to reduce my apprenticeship from the normal four years to three. The four of us were interviewed together in front of the company superintendent in what proved to be a lecture on the great traditions of the company and a pep talk about our behaviour when we got to sea. In less than an hour we were on our way back to Greenhithe clutching our new company hat badges as Ellerman and Bucknall apprentices.

Back on the *Worcester*, at the end of term in December, we were allowed to have an evening meal with Captain Steele and his charming wife before we left on completion of our course. During the evening he showed us his interesting collection of photographs taken during his life at sea. One which remains in my memory was taken showing the very basic toilets on the *Worcester*, featuring five bare bottoms sticking out into the gap between the cubicles and the ship's side!

On the last day, wearing our company badges, all the leavers were given a lift in the truck that carried the cadets' luggage to the Greenhithe railway station, and it was a great moment as we passed all the other cadets walking to the same destination. We were off to sea and schooldays were behind us, or so we thought.

At home it was all hustle and bustle as my mother put together my seagoing gear with all the enthusiasm of a sailor's wife helping her son to follow in his father's footsteps. So much so that when I left to join my first ship in Birkenhead, on the 27th December 1954, I had a full size trunk, two large suitcases, a holdall and a sailor's kitbag which had been made out of canvas by my father. Before that day I had to organise and obtain my indentures (contract for 3 years as an apprentice) signed by my mother and the now retired company secretary of the Hain Line, Mr Cogar, who still lived in St. Ives. My wages were set at £8.50 per month plus my keep. I then awaited the wishes of the Ellerman and Bucknall company superintendent as to which ship I would join.

Just before the Christmas holiday period I received a railway warrant and insturctions to travel to the River Mersey to board the SS *City of Cardiff* on 28th December. This meant I was able to have a very pleasant Christmas at home during which I was presented with a Bible by my local Methodist minister, the Reverend Slater, at the Fore Street chapel.

It was at 2pm on the 27th December that I left my mother standing on St. Ives Station with a woebegone look on her face. My rail journey took seventeen hours and I had to change at St. Erth, Plymouth, Bristol, and Crewe before finally arriving in Birkenhead at 7am the next morning, very weary from dragging my luggage around all those stations. I stopped briefly at a café for some breakfast and by 9am I had loaded my gear into a taxi and arrived at the ship's berth, the west float in the docks.

Berthed alongside and loading a general cargo of machine parts, cars, lorries, beer, whisky, tinned food stuffs and many other varied packages was the SS *City of Cardiff*. The ship was bound for Port Sudan, Aden, Colombo, Calcutta, Chalna and Chittagong via the Suez Canal, and all five of her deep cargo holds were being loaded from the quayside with the aid of two cranes and the ship's own equipment of steam winches and derricks. The noise of the scene was intense, with the rattle of steam banging in the pipes of the winches and the shouts of the dockers instructions mixing with the strong breeze blowing down the quayside. To me it was a picture of real magic as I watched a gang of dockers loading cars into the largest hold, number two, on the foredeck. Unnoticed in the busy scene I paid off my taxi driver and began struggling up the gangway of the partly loaded ship with my suitcases, trunk and other luggage.

Eventually the quartermaster on duty at the gangway called for my fellow apprentice Greg and together we pulled the remaining luggage on board.

It was now I learned an early lesson whilst I stood talking to my new sailing companion. The docker controlling the nearest derricks of number three hold, close to the gangway, called out: "Sorry, my boy, you looked puffed. If you had asked me I would have lifted your gear on board with the cargo and saved you the trouble." First lesson to a greenhorn completed and remembered on many occasions in my life to come – always look to do the job in the easiest way.

Our cabin was a small space in the forward accommodation under the navigating bridge together with the captain's and radio officer's accommodation. The chief, second and third officers, plus the purser/chief steward, lived on the deck below us, which also contained the saloon where meals were served. After unpacking my gear, stowing the suitcases and having a chat with Greg, I was taken to see the Master of the *City of Cardiff*.

Captain Groundwater was well over six feet tall, with a very solemn face and deep brown eyes under bushy eyebrows. His manner, as he sat at his desk, seemed to indicate that he had better things to do than talk to a new first trip apprentice. "Good to see you have arrived safely," was his opening remark then, "see the Chief Officer Mr Graham for your orders and make sure you learn all you can about the ship. Good morning." With that he turned back to writing at his desk and we were dismissed.

Chief Officer Murdo Graham was an entirely different character. He was from Skye, in the Western Isles of Scotland, and talked in a very broad island accent which I always had problems in understanding. However, he instructed my mate Greg to show me around the ship and intoduce me to the other officers and crew.

Thus I commenced my duties by an extensive tour of the ship. The second and third officers were regular hard working deck officers and they were out and about the decks supervising and observing the loading of the general cargo.

The vessel was built in 1942 as a war replacement for the many ships being sunk at that time of conflict with Germany. Its original name was the SS *Empire Spartan*, and the shipyard of William Lithgow in Glasgow had made a fine job building the vessel even though the country was at war and supplies were short at the time. Her overall length was 446 feet long and the beam 56 feet, and fully loaded she had a draft of 26 feet, her gross tonnage was 6987 tons and her deadweight 10,043 tons. While at sea in fine weather the ship would steam some 250 nautical miles at just over 10 knots in twenty-four hours. On the bridge the equipment was basic, with a very old radar that was only switched on in thick fog and when approaching or leaving port, or sometimes in emergency. On a lot of occasions it failed altogether and the radio officer frequently seemed to be trying to repair it; often during his watch in the radio room. A large brass engine telegraph stood close to the shining varnished ship's wheel. At the rear of the bridge were two large telephones: one connected to the captain and navigating officers' cabins and the other to the chief engineer and engine room. Various signal flags and other equipment were stowed around the space as well as a small desk where I would stand and record the engine movements ordered on the telegraph, together with other salient points, as we moved the ship around on sailing and arriving at our destinations. Behind the bridge was a small chart room with the two chronometers which were checked every day by the second officer to enable us to navigate at sea. Four quartermasters were employed to steer the ship; each for six hours a day, and then working at least two more hours on general deck duties. In port the quartermasters kept a gangway watch and helped the duty officer in his duties. All of these men came from islands around the coast of Scotland and were some of the best seamen with whom I served at sea.

The forward accommodation of the ship consisted of the cabins aft of number two hold for the captain navigators, apprentices, radio officer and purser chief steward (who as well as supervising the feeding of the crew helped the captain with the many jobs necessary dealing with paperwork, money and records). In front of this block of accommodation was the ship's saloon with its round portholes looking out on the foredeck of the ship.

Further towards the stern was the number three hold and then a further block of accomodation placed above the engine room and around the ship's funnel. Here six engineers and quartermasters had their cabins, together with a good number of the thirty-six Indian crew. This accommodation was then completed with a large galley and bakehouse which spread right across the ship. Some more of the deck crew lived in the deckhouse at the stern, which again was separated from the galley by holds number four and five.

Standing at the engine room door I looked down in wonder at this amazing space. It was, of course, dominated by the engine itself, looking rather like a straightened pear shape. Stretching from the narrow cylinder at the forward end to the really wide one towards the stern. On the side of the engine were the actual controls for working the ship when manoeuvring at different speeds. Ahead of the engine stood two oil fuelled boilers which provided the steam both to drive the engine and work the various winches used to load and discharge cargo, and also to drive the windlass on foredeck used to hoist the anchors.

After meeting some of the deck crew and finding out about where various items were stored for use at sea, I was, to say the least after my long rail journey, exhausted, and I was really glad to store my clothes, make my bunk and slip between the sheets after my first day at work.

5

Off to Sea at Last

Three days later the total cargo was loaded, the hatches closed and the derricks lowered and locked into place. Then all preparations were made to sail to foreign parts.

On that New Year's Eve in 1954 at Birkenhead, thirteen vessels sailed out through the locks, and the *City of Cardiff* was one of nine British flagged vessels included in that number. In actual fact, our national ships comprised one third of all merchant vessels in the world, a very different situation than that of today.

On sailing, my position was on the bridge and I had an eagle's eye view as the old ship moved slowly out into the River Mersey and navigated her way down the river to the sea. Little did I know then, as I watched with admiration the ship's pilot at work, that I would serve as a ship's pilot for over twenty years later in my life.

After the pilot had disembarked, my seagoing duties began as a bridge lookout and I came on watch at midnight on New Year's Day, 1955. There was no time for celebration, as I was stationed outside on the wing of the bridge staring into the darkness with orders to report any lights or matters of interest I could see. "You will be keeping six hour watches," the chief officer had explained, and I, therefore, as junior apprentice, kept the watch till 6am in the morning. He continued, "We are in restricted waters and there is bad weather forecast for the Bay of Biscay. It will be that way for a while I am afraid." And so it turned out.

In my two watches of six hours on duty I was allowed two breaks of a quarter of an hour, otherwise I stood watching the horizon and reporting any lights, ships or objects in the water. By the 2nd of January we had reached the stormy waters of the Bay of Biscay and the speed of the ship had reduced to less than two knots in the south-west gale.

On the second day of bad weather I was to get a first real test of whether I was suitable for my chosen career. Above the bridge on the *City of Cardiff* stood the signal mast; flimsy in comparison to the main masts of the ship, it carried four signal halliards for displaying messages by flag. It stood, however, above all the other masts and the flag level was some seventy feet above sea level. A small wire ladder, with wooden struts approximately a foot apart, lead to the crosstrees at the top of the mast.

Unfortunately, when taking down the International Code Flag H (which means 'I have a pilot on board'), on leaving the River Mersey, the flag rope had not been secured properly and now, during the afternoon watch, the rope broke free and streamed back over the funnel as the ship battled with the sea and swell.

Rather rashly, the second officer in charge of the watch instructed me to climb the ladder, grasp the halliard and bring the end back down to its proper place. It was a daunting climb and I think the officer was expecting me to refuse.

Anyway, I began the climb and managed to get about half way up when a really large squall of wind and rain buffeted the ship. I was forced to hang on where I was as the ship moved and pitched in the violent wind.

Below me the officer was shouting for me to come back down and leave the job. No doubt he feared I would fall off.

I simply clung on where I was, and after a short period the motion of the ship eased a little and I continued climbing. No way was I going to be beaten, and in due course I grabbed the halliard and came down to the bridge deck. After all, it was me that failed to tie the wretched rope properly in the first place!

I was rewarded with a half hour smoke period after that episode and there was no doubt the second officer looked a very relieved man as I got back to the deck level.

During this time we had one passenger on board in the shape of a large Alsatian dog and it had been kept in the spare accommodation during the storm. Unfortunately it had been sick and made a mess of the cabin. On reaching the calmer waters of the Strait of Gibraltar I had been ordered to take the dog to the deckhouse at the base of the mast on the forward deck of the ship. There it was to be confined, quartered in a kennel made by the ship's carpenter and fed twice a day. However, it was only restrained by a dog lead and soon broke loose and wandered all over the ship. Of course, the two apprentices were then ordered to catch it. As you can imagine, it gave us some good exercise as we chased it, scrambling over and around the windlass and winches and getting really hot and bothered on the way. Eventually we succeeded in catching the dog and it was then restrained by a chain.

In due course, as the new apprentice, I was tasked with cleaning the poor animal, as it had explored all the greasy places it could find and was in a really messy state. "Now lad," said the chief officer, "that dog is to be delivered to its owners in Colombo and you had better get it in a reasonable state by then. After all, you were supposed to tie it up."

My protests were to no avail, and on a fine afternoon I tied the poor dog to the deck, forward of the bridge, and struggled to clean him with a bucket of Teepol and a scrubbing brush. Above me an admiring group of officers cheered me on as the foam from the Teepol covered me, the struggling dog and a good deal of the foredeck as well.

"Good experience for a first trip, apprentice," grunted the chief officer as I reported that I had finished the job.

Two weeks after leaving Birkenhead the *City of Cardiff* sailed into Port Said in Egypt. It was a busy port with many tankers, cargo and passenger ships waiting to join a southbound convoy to take them from the Mediterranean to the Red Sea through the Suez Canal. We were moored on buoys and waited the best part of a day for a northbound convoy of some twenty-five ships to pass into the Mediterranean. Six Egyptians boarded our vessel together with two small mooring boats. These would be used to run ropes ashore in the canal if we had to stop for any reason. The men stayed on deck during our passage and were under the control of the British pilot who boarded just before we moved on.

While we waited, a number of boats came out to us and moored alongside with many goods to sell to the crew. I was shocked to find that to buy a week old copy of the *Sunday Express* I would have to pay two shillings and sixpence (12.5 pence today). As I was only earning eight pounds fifty pence a month I did not buy a copy, although several days later I did get hold of the chief officer's copy without payment. These boats were called bum boats by the crew and some of their owners were pretty good entertainers while they tried to sell their leather, textile and plastic goods.

Eventually I was at my station on the bridge as the ship took her place in a southbound convoy and we were on our way to the Bitter Lakes near Ismailia. I was keeping a six hour watch as we proceeded southwards.

In the sunshine of the early afternoon I marvelled at the amazing spectacle of the straight canal as we steamed along. It was possible from the waterway ahead to make out the curve of the earth's surface, where the canal stretched into the far distance. Along the way small neat white buildings marked the signal stations controlling the movement of ships, and the canal side was marked with kilometre marks along its full length. Apart from recording these stations in the movement book, I shared the task with the officer on the bridge of noting any morse lamplight signals from the ship ahead of us showing instructions to slow down or stop if required (no radios on the bridge in those days to talk to the vessel ahead or astern).

Soon we were in the Bitter Lakes and the British pilot was replaced by a Frenchman to take us on to the port of Suez . Here also, we waited for another northbound convoy to pass before we continued.

One thing I did find difficult was trying to sleep when off watch. The night was very hot and continually interrupted by loud chirping crickets which boarded at Port Said and disappeared again at Suez.

It was some forty-eight hours after arriving in Egypt before we dropped the pilot and began to steam through the Gulf of Suez.

Here the cliffs could be seen on either side of the gulf and the bright hot sunlight clearly showed the browns, purples yellows and blacks of the rock formations in these desert lands. On board, our uniform white shorts and shirts were soon ringing in sweat as we kept watch for the numerous large vessels making their way up to the canal. Conditions on board were made much worse by the gentle following wind which was reduced by the ship's forward speed and left us gasping for air in the intense heat. Soon we passed the Brothers Lighthouse, which stands at the entrance to the Gulf of Suez, and entered into the wider regions of the Red Sea. Now the apprentices were back on day work, and it was quite a relief to dress in light working clothes.

Three days later an English pilot boarded the ship to guide us into Port Sudan, situated roughly half way down the Red Sea and the destination of some 500 tons of the cargo. Most of this was made up of beer and spirits carried in special secure spaces in two of the hatches. Our duty at this time was to share with the second and third officers on watch to see this cargo was not stolen, or indeed imbibed while being discharged. To this end we were also assisted by the quartermasters as not one of us could stand the intense heat of the ship's hold for more than thirty minutes. However, the Sudanese dockers, with their massive heads of curly hair, cheerfully worked away in these conditions without noticing the heat.

I did get a much needed break over lunchtime when I visited the the Flying Angel Mission for a cool drink and a rest. Port Sudan itself was remarkable for the clear blue water, and looking over the side of the ship an amazing array of fish could be seen, which the Indian crew were soon catching for their evening meal.

After a twelve hour stay we were on our way south again and some three days later we approached the southernmost entrance to the Red Sea. Here the land narrowed in on either side and in the middle of the waterway were a set of rocky barren islands. The largest of these being Perim, where once a coaling station

Eric in new cadet's uniform joining HMS *Worcester*.

HMS *Worcester* – Eric's training ship.

The Cornish cadets on board HMS *Worcester*, 1954.
Eric fourth from left.

Changing for a rugby match in the cadet's sleeping area, 1954.
Possession chests were our only permanent space on the ship.

Rugby team on board HMS *Worcester*.
Eric second from right on back row.

Coming 2nd in the 220 yard race HMS *Worcester*, sports day.
Eric in left lane.

The cadets marching on sports day.

Duke of Edinburgh inspects cadets on HMS *Worcester*.
Eric with cap pushed down in back row 10th from end.

City of Newcastle berthed in London.

MV *Jack Wharton* in Newlyn.
A vessel managed by Everard in later years.

MV *Gardience*, on a regular trip to Hayle power station delivering coal from South Wales.

was situated to refuel steamers with fresh supplies of coal. However, that day was past, and the island slipped by almost unnoticed.

Now out of the Red Sea and steaming the short distance to Aden, the wind was at last blowing across the ship, and we had some relief from the searing heat of the previous ten days.

Aden itself was a barren, hilly and interesting port to enter. The blue sea was a strange contrast against the dark brown of the high land around the town. The harbour was very busy, and moored to buoys in the roads we were soon discharging our small amount of cargo and receiving fuel and stores from an array of small craft. On shore the shops and bazaars were mainly run by Indians and bargains abounded in many goods which could be bought as presents for those at home; but it was only a lucky few who could go ashore to buy them.

All too soon we were on our way eastwards once more, heading across the Indian ocean towards Colombo in Ceylon, or Sri Lanka as it is now called. There we were able to have a good run ashore as we stayed for three days to discharge well over a thousand tons of goods.

It was here that I first tasted Chinese food. In actual fact it took two visits, as on the first visit I took fright at the food on tables around me and ordered ham and eggs. Nevertheless, my fellow apprentice persuaded me to return on the second night, and I did order a meal which included fried prawns; I was hooked after that. By now my working routine was well established and I was really enjoying myself in my chosen profession. Nevertheless, I was soon to have a lesson in the reality of trading with the poorer nations of the world at that time.

It was about a week later that the *City of Cardiff* anchored outside the River Hooghly awaiting our turn to proceed up the one hundred and twenty miles or so of waterway to Calcutta, as it was then called. Around us some thirty ships waited and watched the graceful white pilot vessel for the signal of the arrival of their pilot to guide them up the river. All the major shipping companies trading to India experienced this wait at some time. There was no sign of land, just a marker buoy to

49

e

indicate the start of the river passage. As far as the eye could see the water was a dirty brown colour, discolouring the blue waters of the Indian Ocean.

We waited a frustrating two weeks before a small tender put out from the pilot vessel carrying a smart Indian gentleman in a western style dress and his Indian cook with all his own cooking utensils and food.

Both apprentices, together with the third officer, met the pilot at the top of the pilot ladder. While he was escorted to the captain's cabin by the third officer, we remained to help the cook fetch the luggage and equipment on board. To my surprise (it was during the early afternoon) the pilot spent a good half hour with Captain Groundwater in his cabin having a drink, before retiring to the cabin reserved for him for an afternoon nap.

Some three hours later we hove up the anchor and proceeded to the first anchorage. Indeed it was to take nearly three days to pass the shallow parts of the river and arrive in the port of Calcutta.

As we made our way up the Hooghly, I was to learn just how different the harsh conditions of living in India were at that time. Just inside the actual entrance to the river is the village of Diamond Harbour and the channel at this point passes very close to the river bank. I was on watch as lookout and recorder of the ship's movements as we approached this stretch of water. As I looked, a partly decomposed human body floated past the ship and I, of couse, hurried to report to the pilot and the officer of the watch what I had seen.

To my intense surprise the pilot dismissed my report with a laugh. "That's nothing on this river," he said. "Look, we are just coming close to the village of Diamond Harbour and you no doubt can see that large crowd of people over there standing near to the bank."

"Yes," I said.

"Well, they have been there for the past three days, and as we approach you will see an old boy lying on a bier. If you watch carefully you will see him move from time to time. They are waiting for him to die so that they can incinerate the funeral pyre."

I looked on in horror as we passed, and it was just as the pilot reported.

On arrival in Calcutta we moored on buoys out in the river. It was to take us eight hours to secure the anchors and break the heavy anchor chains away and make them fast to the buoys backed up with heavy wires, so that we were safe from the massive bore tides which affected the port every fortnight or so. The wave of our own bore tide on the Severn looked very small against the waves that ran all the way up past the mooring we had secured in the river on our arrival. We were to spend ten days there before taking another six hours or so to dismantle our moorings and move in through the riverside locks to Kiddepore docks.

Then, after another week, we finished discharging the bulk of our cargo and began loading Indian goods including ore and large bundles of sacking material called gunnies for Dundee, Antwerp and Rotterdam.

Next on to Chalna and Chittagong near the Burmese boarder in East Pakistan (now called Bangladesh) where we discharged the last of our outward cargo and commenced loading bales of jute used in the production of sacking.

Onward then to Visakhapatnam, a very interesting port nearly 400 miles south-west of Calcutta. Here the cliffs along the coastline are very high and the port is hidden behind them and it is only possible to enter by way of a narrow channel dominated by the high land on either side. Running along the coast was a very heavy sea swell and this made it difficult to get the Indian pilot on board, and with the ship rolling heavily it was quite a heart-stopping moment as we slipped through the narrow entrance. Here, behind these high cliffs, was a busy hive of industry, with a large shipyard building modern ships for the Indian Merchant Navy, as well as jetties where ships like the *City of Cardiff* loaded and discharged cargoes.

Then on to Ceylon and the Port of Galle in the south of the island where thousands of chests of tea were loaded to complete our homeward cargo.

Now we started the long journey home, retracing the passage

through the Indian Ocean to Aden, on through the Red Sea to the Suez canal, thence the Mediterranean, with the final stretch along the coasts of Portugal and Spain, through the English Channel and North Sea to Dundee in Scotland.

The voyage had taken four months and I was very keen to go home. Unfortunately, I had to stay as the ship steamed around the continent, and I finally left for home in Antwerp at the end of April 1955.

I must admit that the train journey from Paddington to St. Ives was one of mounting exicitment for me. As the train travelled westward I was full of impatience to get back to Cornwall, and the long haul from Newton Abbot to Plymouth, across the southern fringes of Dartmoor, seemed never ending. After leaving Plymouth North Road Station, the satisfaction of being back in my homeland as we crossed the Royal Albert Bridge over the River Tamar, was a feeling I was not to lose in all my days at sea. The final run from Camborne to St. Erth and then on to the St. Ives branch-line was the most satisfying of all. I counted the small coasters in the port of Hayle and looked at the blue waters of St. Ives Bay. Then it was on to my mother standing on the station platform to greet me at the start of a month's leave.

6

An Elephant as Cargo

All too soon the letter arrived from the company containing the order to join the SS *City of Portsmouth* in Newport, South Wales. This vessel was an American built Liberty vessel in 1943 of 7,208 gross tons and called the SS *Samhain* until Ellerman's renamed it at the end of the war. In fact, the USA was producing one of these ships a day during the war and many British companies acquired them at the end of the war to rebuild their fleets following wartime losses. My father's first command in the Andrew Weir company was one such vessel; the SS *Rowanbank*. Ellerman Lines owned ten similar vessels in 1955.

As I arrived at my new ship I was delighted to find that I was no longer the junior apprentice, but number three of four, while the senior apprentice was Craig Rich, who was later to become known to BBC West of England television viewers for many years as their weather forecaster.

The SS *City of Portsmouth* was on a slightly longer voyage than my first trip to India, calling at Karachi in West Pakistan as well as Bombay, before discharging in Ceylon and East Indian ports. Nevertheless, we all expected to be home in time for some Christmas leave, something which we did indeed looked forward to.

We soon began to work as a good team, and some eight weeks later we arrived in Calcutta, where the junior apprentice and myself were in for a rude shock!

53

As the ship docked we could see, well in the distance, another City Line vessel, and this proved to be a sister ship, the SS *City of Stafford,* 7,200 gross tons, ex SS *Sam Torch.*

Soon after we were moored in the river, Craig Rich arrived at our cabin to announce that the two junior apprentices were to be transferred to the *City of Stafford* the next day. This was bad news for our Christmas as the ship was engaged in the Canada to India service and not expected to be home for at least another nine months or so. We spent the rest of the day packing our cases, and the very next day transferred to the *City of Stafford.*

After signing on at the Calcutta shipping office we were taken by taxi down to the Kidderpore dock. Here we could see the cargo being discharged from Canada and the United States; consisting of machinery, tractors, lorries and even powdered milk delivered as aid to India. The main difference between the two ships though, was this ship carried only two apprentices; so in double quick time I had aspired to senior apprentice.

A week later we began loading cargo for Saint John, New Brunswick in the Bay of Fundy, Quebec, Three Rivers and Montreal in the St. Lawrence River in Canada. Fully loaded the *City of Stafford* could carry over 10,000 tons of cargo, but on this run rarely carried that much. On this occasion we loaded 4,000 tons of gunnies, tea and jute before sailing to Chittagong once more, to load a further 2,000 tons of similar cargo. Then we sailed back across the Indian Ocean to Madras where the loading was due to be completed for Canada.

The *City of Stafford* was a little faster than the *City of Portsmouth,* averaging approximately two hundred and sixty-four sea miles on a day's run. The crew was made up of thirteen Europeans and thirty-five Indians recruited in Calcutta. The master of the ship was a real gentleman called Captain Astbury and he had his wife on board for the voyage.

It was in early September that we sailed from Madras bound for Canada, when we received a surprising radio message from the company. It read: 'Proceed to Cochin at best speed to load an elephant for transit to Montreal.'

Cochin was a small delightful port on the west coast of India in the state of Kerala. It was fairly close to the most southern point of India. It transpired that a small boy living in a town called Granby, some hundred miles south-east of Montreal, had written to the Prime Minister of India, Pandit Nehru, from his school and told him that he had never seen an elephant. The Prime Minister immediately ordered that an elephant be sent to Granby where the local zoo would take delivery of it. The *City of Stafford* happened to be the closest ship to the port actually bound for Canada.

We arrived to a reception party on the jetty consisting of local State Ministers, the Canadian Ambassador and the press. Indian and Canadian flags were flying in many places and a band was playing.

The chief officer had designated the two apprentices to work with the ship's carpenter to build a covered shelter in a position by number four hold, where the ship's accommodation would give the animal some shelter from spray in headwinds. So we had prepared a wooden floor and had three sheltering bulkheads (walls) with one side open to allow the animal's carer to feed and tend it. Waiting on the hatch itself were the beams and timber to cover this shelter as soon as the animal was on board.

Soon after the ship had come alongside, a senior politician made a speech and the band played the National Anthems of the two nations. Then, caged in a wooden box, a quayside crane lifted the elephant 'Ambika' on to the ship's afterdeck close to the number four hold.

To say the least, the elephant totally disliked the whole performance! She had been happily eating a supply of bamboo left near her cage and meant for food on the voyage, and suddenly finding herself swinging through the air was not at all to her liking. As she was lifted into the air she squealed, trumpeted and showered the whole quay with dung, sending the Indian and Canadian guests running for cover.

Following that performance the Chief Minister of Kerala, the Canadian Ambassador, several Indian members of parliament, not to mention local dignitaries, tried to regain their composure and come up the steps of the ship's gangway with some dignity.

They then all disappeared to the saloon for drinks while the carpenter, myself and fellow apprentice toiled to complete the shelter for a very unhappy elephant.

All went well at first, and I must admit I was lulled into complacency. Chippy (ships' nickname for the carpenter) was now on the roof of the shelter and nailing it down to withstand future Atlantic weather. As I stretched to hand him nails and wood Ambika suddenly lashed out with her trunk and sent me flying across the deck to land against the steel bulwark of the ship.

Thank goodness the press and officers were with the partygoers and they did not know of my accident, and no picture exists of me being carried to my bunk for the rest of the day. It was a fact that after this incident I treated Ambika with extra due care and respect on our voyage halfway round the world.

Eventually our reluctant passenger was installed in her shelter, and the next day, as soon as we had loaded a small amount of cargo, we were on our way once more across the Indian Ocean.

The passage to Aden was achieved without incident, although we did have to ration the elephant's food as she had eaten so much at Cochin. We mangaged though, by sending a message ahead to Port Said, to get some more food for Ambika for the rest of the voyage. So it was in mid September we set out from Egypt to Saint John in New Brunswick, Canada.

Our problems really began halfway across the Atlantic when a hurricane moved out of the Gulf of New Orleans and headed across our path. As the weather worsened and a steep swell came up from the west, Captain Asbury slowed the ship, and by heading on a southwesterly course allowed the centre of the storm to pass ahead of us. Even so, we had to contend with some very bad weather, with waves breaking onto the foredeck and the old ship shuddering under the force of the swell.

Ambika was suffering at this time, like the rest of us, and decided that the best way to end it was to break out of her shelter. So with some force she managed to break free fom her restraining ropes and, as the ship slammed into the next swell, the pitching around caused the elephant to slide pell-mell down the deck and

56

jam herself in the starboard alleyway. This connected the fore and afterdeck around the ship's accommodation.

Soon the keeper, three deck officers, the carpenter, myself and my fellow apprentice were battling with ropes to secure the animal and save her from further danger. This was achieved fairly easily as the elephant was unable to move freely. We then had to decide what to do next, bearing in mind the weather was getting worse and clearly we could not wait for an improvement. So under the chief officer's orders we got power on to the starboard number four hatch winch (normally used for lifting cargo on and off the ship), and with two heavy ropes around Ambika's back legs going to the winch, and two more around her neck and secured to a bollard, we took up the slack on the back legs and eased the neck rope. As the ship climbed the next steep wave, with the help of the ropes on her back legs, we were able to ease the distressed animal out of the alleyway, and with each succeeding wave inch her across the deck until we had her back in her shelter. It was to take nearly three hours and all of us, including the elephant, were exhausted by the end of the saga.

In due course we cleared the bad weather only to get a further hurricane warning from the Caribbean that another storm was on its way. Needless to say, under the captain's urging, the chief engineer opened our steam engine to full speed and at nearly twelve knots we arrived in the Bay of Fundy ahead of the bad weather.

Following our arrival in Saint John, New Brunswick the bad weather from the hurricane was upon us and within twelve hours it was snowing heavily.

Poor Ambika was suffering from the cold and it was decided to discharge the animal and send her by train to Granby. To get her ashore proved very simple; the tides in the Bay of Fundy are the biggest in the world and the water alongside the berth was lifting the ship from thirty feet below the quay to thirty feet above it at high water. So we waited for the ship to level with the quay and then simply laid boards from the deck to the land and Ambika's keeper led her off the ship and into a waiting enclosed railway truck. She gave no trouble at all. She seemed to know that the hateful voyage was over and the best thing to do was to co-operate.

Two weeks later I was lucky to be one of an official party to travel from Montreal to Granby to see Ambika in her new surroundings. We enjoyed the hospitality of our hosts very much, but when we entered the elephant house at the zoo, Ambika rose up on her hind legs, lashed her trunk in a fury and trumpeted her dislike of these sailors who had given her such a bad time at sea. Oh well, they say 'an elephant never forgets'. There followed a very pleasant meal and a visit to a nightclub before we returned to the ship.

During our time in the St. Lawrence river we were to see some very wonderful scenery. The colours of the fall were magnificent, with purples, browns, yellows, greens and even blacks blending together in their breathtaking beauty. We visited the riverside ports of Three Rivers, and the city of Quebec in which we saw the battleground at the Heights of Abraham where General Wolfe stormed the cliffs above the city. However, the most spectacular trip of all was our passage up the Saguenay River to Port Alfred. This tributary flows through narrow channels between really high cliffs and was a wonderful experience for a young apprentice. One particular part of the passage really remains strong in my memory. On leaving Port Alfred we proceeded at night and, as we travelled between the cliffs of the river, our pilot would order a long blast on the whistle and this would reverberate around the ship as a loud mournful reminder that soon we would be on our way back to the heat and noise of India.

We finally completed loading our mainly aid cargo at Montreal and on the 19th October we were heading downriver on our way once more. All too soon our pilot left us near Mont Louis at a small headland called Father Point, and then we set off to cross the north Atlantic towards our next destination.

It was at that point that I was, I must admit, at my most miserable, and the next day while working with my brother apprentice we discussed how to get off the ship by feigning sickness. As we were making a count of the mates stores we found an old edition of a book called the *Ship Captain's Medical*

Guide. My partner then dared me to pretend that I had an appendicitis, and as foolish youths of eighteen sometimes will, I took him up on the dare. Now I only look on my foolish actions as stupid and I realise I was extremely lucky to get away with my plan.

On reading the book I discovered that at first the sufferer has a pain right across his stomach, so with some good acting I complained to the chief steward, Dudley, that I had such a pain and retired to my bunk at about two in the afternoon. At four o'clock the chief steward came up with some medicine for an aching bowel. However, by five o'clock I was complaining that the pain had gone into my right side just above the leg.

All too soon the captain arrived at the cabin to assess the situation. Captain Asbury was very concerned and told me that he was getting some advice from the Canadian Coastguard as to what to do with me. About an hour later he arrived back in the cabin with the news that the ship had altered course to arrive at St. John's, Newfoundland where I would be examined by a doctor and operated on if need be. It also transpired that an American Coast Guard cutter was making for our position, and if they had caught up with us I would have been operated on at sea and probably returned to our ship.

As it was we arrived in St. John's and by this time I was a mighty worried apprentice. The chief officer had given me a lecture; I think he suspected what was going on and said he had to undo many of the preparations for the ship's passage across the Atlantic, and heaven help me if there was nothing wrong with me!

Well, the result of all this stress and worry produced a high temperature and the doctor who came on board confirmed the diagnosis. So there I was on my way to hospital. Next day they operated without any comment to me and it could well have been by then a genuine case of appendicitis.

A fortnight later I was a passenger on a Furness Withy passenger ship called the MV *Nova Scotia* bound for Liverpool. It was a silly and wicked thing to do and I still remember my worries as the *City of Stafford* raced back to the capital city of Newfoundland.

7

A Very Unhappy Apprentice

After a short leave at home I found myself posted to the *City of Pretoria*, then loading in London's West India docks for South Africa. As the vessel was not sailing until the New Year I was delighted that it appeared I was to be in the UK over Christmas. I should have remembered never to 'count my chickens' – or Christmas holidays!

As it happened I was in for a real shock. On the 19th of December I was summoned to the captain's cabin and told I was to join the *City of Johannesburg*, a twelve passenger vessel then berthed in Glasgow. I soon discovered from the maritime press that the vessel was engaged in a round the world voyage and, to my disgust, sailing on Christmas Eve.

So it was that on the 21st December I boarded this remarkable ship which was to be my home, apart from leave periods, for the next sixteen months. Built at the yard of Barclay Curle in Glasgow and having a gross tonnage of 8,207 tons the ship had been intended to be one of six ships built for Ellerman Lines all of the same class. However, all the others were steamships while this vessel was driven by two Doxford diesel engines giving a speed of fifteen knots. I understood that Sir John Ellerman had changed her profile to his own needs and had travelled to South Africa and back on a number of occasions. The vessel was, in effect, in a class of her own, and I really admired this splendid ship as I boarded at the berth in the River Clyde. I was met by the other apprentice, Michael Crewe, a South African with whom I shared a cabin at boat deck level beneath the bridge. Michael proved a good mate and soon filled me in on the ship's officers with whom we were going to serve on this remarkable voyage.

The captain, as I recall, was called Marchant and was a rather ill-tempered man who suffered from poor health. He seemed to think that apprentices were there to be seen and not heard and only spoke to us if it were to give an order or a telling off, the latter of which I had more than a few.

The chief officer was known as 'Mad Robbie' and he would explode into bad-tempered tantrums without any warning whatsoever. He was to break my spirit before the voyage was out, but I was all enthusiasm as he dealt out the first day's work. The second and third officers were very easy-going and helpful.

Seven engineers, an electrical officer, radio officer and purser, chief steward, stewardess, carpenter and four quartermasters made up the European part of the crew. While the rest of the crew consisted of forty-two Indians who were mainly Hindu or Muslim.

At this time in 1955 the weather was really bad in the North Atlantic and continuous storms had been battering Scotland for the previous week. The ship had completed loading three thousand tons of earth ballast in the holds to help submerge the propellers under the water so that it was better able to make progress in the bad winter weather.

Michael Crewe and myself were instructed to tally and check the voyage stores as they were brought aboard. The Indian storekeeper and three crewmen were engaged in storing the various drums of paint, cleaning fluids, linseed oil and all the implements that the ship needed in the store under the foredeck near the bow. It was on this very task that Michael and I fell foul of both the captain and the chief officer because, not being very experienced, we did not think to check the stowage of the stores or the lashings to keep them in place on the shelves within the store, and to be fair to us the deck officers did not check the stowage either.

It was on the evening of the 23rd December that the Ellerman shore superintendent wished us a Happy Christmas and described how he was away home to enjoy the festive season as he stepped onto solid ground.

Finally, during a lull in the weather, the *City of Johannesburg* slipped her moorings, and with the help of two harbour tugs sailed away down the River Clyde to load paper and other general cargo in Eastern Canada and the United States. The ship was then bound for the Philippines, Japan, Hong Kong, and Communist China by way of the Panama Canal. From there we would be loading in the ports of Eastern Asia before crossing the Indian Ocean and travelling through the Suez Canal on the way to the United Kingdom to complete a round the world voyage. A very exciting prospect for a teenager looking for adventure and keen to see the world.

It was not long before my illusions were to be rudely shaken. Within twelve hours the ship had cleared the coast of Northern Ireland and had run into a massive angry sea with a considerable swell, all driven on by a deep depression, with severe gale force winds and driving rain. The vessel's speed soon slowed and Captain Marchant was forced to slow the ship further to avoid damage from the huge waves breaking over the decks.

On Christmas morning I awoke to find our cabin floor flooded with seawater and our clothes all damp and uncomfortable due to the prevailing conditions in the accommodation. No hot food was available, only sandwiches and cups of tea and coffee. To say it was a miserable start to Christmas was an understatement. The bad weather did not improve during the day and over the twenty-fours hours we only steamed 48 nautical miles towards our destination (with navigation in such circumstances being at best a dead reckoning guess). Keeping watches of six hours on and six hours off, continually having to brace oneself against the violent motion of the ship, plus the lack of hot food, soon made us all very tired, and our senior officers rather bad tempered.

Boxing Day proved no better, and as the storm continued tempers became even more frayed. There were other troubles caused by the bad weather and cabins were continually flooded. Meanwhile the ship also sustained some damage to the deck equipment.

Then on the day following Boxing Day it was noticed that the ship's rolling motion had become more extreme, and a check was ordered to see if any compartment had suffered a leak in the severe weather. As it turned out it was not a leak but, in the foredeck stores, all the paint and cleaning fluids, together with the voyage stores, had tumbled out of their stowage spaces and were now sloshing about as a thick purple liquid and adding to the ship's movement. Of course, we two apprentices were on the carpet in front of the captain and chief officer and, despite our protests, received a really good ticking off and a lecture on seamanship. In the meantime the ship had been forced to stop with her engines just turning over to keep her heading into the storm.

Then the chief officer ordered us to accompany the ship's carpenter up on to the foredeck and help him crank a long handle pump to draw this unholy mess out of the store on to the deck. Before we knew it the purple mess ran out onto the foredeck and was blown by the very strong headwind back over the ship's white accommodation and the bridge windows, making it very difficult to keep a lookout, and causing the ship to be renamed by some of the crew as the 'Purple People Eater'. In truth the chief officer was only too aware that the captain was blaming him and in turn he took it out on us. It did not help that the carpenter, who was always complaining that he never made much overtime money, had negotiated a really good deal for doing the job of four hours' overtime for each hour worked. So I had got off on the wrong foot and was to continue in trouble for the rest of the voyage.

In due course the weather eased, and then as we approached Newfoundland it became very cold indeed. We arrived outside the port of Cornerbrook early in the New Year, only to find that the river approach was covered with floating ice. The ship was built for warmer waters, and as we pushed up the waterway behind a small ice breaker the loose ice removed all the paint from the waterline, exposing the white metal underneath. It took us six hours of manoeuvring, with all of us at our stations in the intense cold, to get alongside a riverside jetty.

At this time we were in the captain's bad books, and when the order for an issue of brandy was given to the ship's officers the two apprentices didn't get any.

Cornerbrook had just become a city in 1957 and was completely covered in snow and ice. However, despite our lack of brandy, we did enjoy a Christmas dinner together during a New Year's party after our arrival following that really bad passage from Glasgow.

Our cargo from this port was a consignment of paper for two ports in Japan, and two days later we edged our way out of the river and proceeded southwards (across the entrance to the St. Lawrence River which was now completely frozen and closed to navigation) to the Bay of Fundy and the port of Saint John, New Brunswick.

As we travelled into slightly warmer weather the damage done by the ice became apparent. Pipes which carried water around the ship suddenly sprouted leaks in all directions and we had to help the carpenter once more in a never ending task of repairing them.

At Saint John we received more paint and other deck stores and the crew were able to restore the gleaming white of the accommodation and repaint the decks and other structures to their normal colours, getting rid of the awful purple colour which had covered everything.

After loading more general cargo for the Far East we proceeded to Boston, where I was to learn a useful piece of information at my fellow apprentice's cost. On arrival alongside all crew members were called to interviews with immigration, customs and coastguard officials. I indeed learned that it is extremely rare that any American border official has a sense of humour, and that it was disastrous to assume they had. We waited in a long queue for a considerable time until it was our turn to be examined under the so-called McCarthy Act to see if we had communist sympathies, and until this examination was complete the ship was not allowed to carry out any of its commercial activities. This followed the fact that the ship had visited China and was due to do so again.

When Michael arrived at the desk of an immigration officer he was rather fed up with the long delay, and when asked if he had been to Russia or been a member of the Communist Party replied that he had been to that country. He then produced a fur cap out of his pocket. "This," he announced with gusto, "was given to me by their Prime Minister."

A long delay followed, with the official consulting with others in the room, then a form was filled in and Michael was informed that he would not be allowed ashore in any American port during our stay.

As a result, we then had an armed American guard on the gangway with a Geiger counter to check the rest of us when we did go ashore. Captain Marchant and Mad Robbie were not amused, and although I was not involved I still had some of the blame for this event.

Three days later we moved on to New York, where the guard was still on the gangway and Michael was not allowed ashore. After some time the ship's agent was able to talk to someone in authority and my partner was allowed ashore after he had apologised for his behaviour.

Then the *City of Johannesburg* continued on her way southwards to Philadelphia, Baltimore and Newport News. At the last of these ports fate was once more to take a hand on the events of this voyage.

We had to wait four days on a lay-by berth before loading four thousand tons of coal for Osaka in Japan. On the third night the senior engineers decided to have a run ashore, and the second engineer left a junior officer in charge. His sole duty was to watch the main generator and to deal with any unlikely emergency.

The engineers had a fine night ashore and returned to the ship slightly merry. At the gangway, by way of conversation, the second engineer remarked, "Well, the lights are on, anyway, all should be well." This remark was overheard by the watchman who then informed the merry gentlemen that the lights had gone out at about ten o'clock after a loud explosion in the engine room and they had been out for about an hour.

Minutes later a dismayed second engineer was looking down from the doorway to the engine room at the chief engineer and the unfortunate junior, both picking up pieces of the generator. I must say he never did tell us what was said but there was a prolonged silence between the engineers at mealtimes for a couple of weeks after this incident.

Due to the generator needing replacing, instead of proceeding on southwards towards the Panama Canal we were ordered to return to New York after loading our cargo of coal. We waited at a wharf in Brooklyn for two weeks while a new generator was shipped out on the RMS *Queen Elizabeth*. During this time we has some wonderful nights ashore in Manhattan. My days, however, were spoiled by the boring jobs the chief officer kept giving me.

After a couple of days a gang of American engineers boarded our vessel and were engaged in removing the damaged generator. At the time my main job was polishing brasswork around the ship and I was usually looking for any diversion to get myself off the job for a while. In due course the engineers placed the broken machinery on deck and were making preparations to lift it off onto the wharf.

The American foreman of the gang was a very large man with ginger hair and quite a temper. I usually had a chat with him and we had become friends. On this day I was passing by number four hatch as the foreman was organising his men to use the derricks of our ship to lift the generator. His men were reluctant to drive the ship's winches and I was asked if I could help. Knowing the reluctance of the chief officer to trust me with anything, I agreed without seeking permission.

As luck would have it, I was caught in the act, and had a very public dressing down in front of the American foreman. Following that the gentleman very politely asked mad Robbie if he could see him somewhere private and they disappeared up to the chief officer's cabin. The foreman was to tell me later that he had threatened the mate with extreme violence if he as much as started to treat 'that young apprentice in that way again'. Furthermore he would organise a strike against the ship if he observed any further bullying.

I did not receive any further instructions for work during our stay in the port and was left to get on with the work I had already been told to do.

However, after we sailed with our new generator I was called up to Robbie's cabin and told my fortune in no uncertain manner. His remarks went something like this: "After we get through the Panama Canal I am going to teach you the lesson of your life. We shall be at sea for twenty-eight days and at the end of that time you'll wish you had never been born, let alone sailed on this ship."

So I was left in misery for the next ten days as we sailed south to the island of Curaco in Venezuela. Here, on a wharf which had a view of a castle that we were told had connections with the English Pirate Henry Morgan, we obtained a full load of fuel in order to cross the Pacific.

The beauty of it was lost on me, worried as I was with the promised punishment by the chief officer. In fact, even though I was very impressed by the passage through the Panama Canal, I was so downhearted I did not go ashore for a night's stay in Balboa at the entrance to the Pacific, where it was fiesta time.

The next morning, after we had left on our passage to Manila in the Philippines, I was called to the chief officer's cabin before we turned to our day's work. Michael was ordered to work around the bridge where he would pick up knowledge of navigation etcetera, and I was given my new work orders.

I was issued with a package of emery paper and then told to accompany the ship's officer to the boat deck. Although the Indian crew holystoned the wooden deck most mornings, seawater regularly got into the cracks and edges of the wood and then the steel deck below would rust and the stains would become permanent in the wood itself. In this process the spreading rust was present right through the wood. I was told to attack the rust patches with the emery paper until they had disappeared.

Mad Robbie knew he had given me an impossible task. However much rust I removed the stains remained in the wood. I would have to have destroyed the wood itself to get rid of it. Too frightened to protest, I spent a terrible month on my knees suffering the taunts of the mate who would accuse me of not working hard enough.

Following our arrival in Manila I was back on cargo watch when in port and lookout duty when around the waters of the Far East. That was far better than the drudgery and pressure of the voyage across the Pacific.

8

In More Trouble!

After Manila, we proceeded to the Japanese ports of Yokohama, Nagoya, Osaka and Kobe. (I was much impressed by the price of presents for home with nearly 1500 yen to the pound.) Then we moved on to Hong Kong where a large Royal Navy presence was based.

In the harbour were two aircraft carriers and numerous destroyers. During our short stay a British intelligence officer came and had an interview with the captain and deck officers. Our next two ports were Shanghai and Sing Tao and he explained that the security services were very interested in a vessel being built behind bamboo screens on the way upriver to Shanghai. If the officers observed anything they were asked to report on it on their return to Hong Kong. As for the second port of Sing Tao, there would be a Chinese naval presence there and any information would prove very useful. Events in Korea at that time were still a major worry.

An adventure indeed, and it became apparent how difficult the area had become when we approached the pilot station outside the River Yangtze. Twelve armed soldiers together with a stout grim officer, carrying a great deal of braid on the shoulder of his immaculate uniform, and a Chinese interpreter, all accompanied the pilot on boarding. These men carried out a search of every cabin in the ship on our way upriver; and took away all personal radios and the ship's signal lamp. For good measure they sealed the radio room for the whole time of our stay in China. Then they moved into the passenger lounge and took it over while on board.

On our passage up the river we were all keenly looking for the bamboo screens, and sure enough there they were. As luck would have it some of the screens had blown down and we were able to see a rather ordinary coastal patrol boat standing in a small boatyard. It had been decided that all of us should try and remember what we had seen, and on our arrival we would draw a composite picture of the vessel.

On coming alongside our riverside berth we were told that the first day would be used to clear the ship and crew before any work could begin. Each of us was searched and our cabins were searched once more, and all papers checked. However, unlike the Americans, this time all of us received permission to go ashore under supervision of a Chinese guide.

During the evening the officers had a meeting in the third officer's cabin while I kept watch, they drew a picture of the vessel behind the bamboo barriers. In due course it was delivered to the officer in Hong Kong without being discovered.

Next morning, promptly at six-thirty, the Chinese dockers boarded the ship to begin to load the general cargo. However, at seven o'clock all work stopped, when a battery of loudspeakers rigged on the quay began playing the *Blue Danube* waltz. All very pleasant we thought, but then a Chinese announcer began broadcasting over the system for about ten minutes before it closed down. Much to our amusement the dock workers now commenced chasing around the cargo spaces with rolled up paper in their hands swatting flies. Our Chinese interpreter told us that the message repeated a good few times in the previous broadcast had been: "If you see a fly, kill a fly!" – this the men were doing. Eventually the whole exercise had to be called off because no work to load the cargo was being done.

There followed another incident just four days later which was even more bizarre to say the least. Several of our European crew wanted to have a football match with another ship. On asking the interpreter if this was possible, we were informed that the authorites would provide us with a first class pitch, and if required football shirts to go with it. We accepted their offer, of course, but then there was the problem of which ship's crew could raise a team and how would we communicate with them?

Out in the river, a quarter of a mile away and berthed on buoys, was a P&O cargo liner; but we had no way of asking the crew whether they could raise a team. After some negotiations with our guards they agreed to let one representative go with the interpreter in a sampan to the P&O ship, but no warning was given of our intended visit. On reaching the accommodation ladder, negotiations were held between the guards on the other vessel and our interpreter. It was agreed that I would be allowed to go halfway up to the main deck, and one of their apprentices could come down to meet me just this once.

So we met as agreed, without anyone listening to our conversation. It was immediately apparent that there was quite a problem because the other apprentice could not tell me whether he could raise a team or not until he asked around the ship. Unfortunately I was not allowed to stay and wait for the answer. In whispers, my opposite number asked, "Have the guards taken your deck torches?"

I was able to say we still had them.

"I will call you at midnight," he said, "from our upper deck, in morse code, with a torch."

"OK," I said, "I will be on our bridge deck and answer you from there."

We shook hands and I came back down aboard the sampan and returned to our ship. It seemed odd that I was not asked what had transpired in our conversation.

Our ship was working an all night shift on loading the cargo and as I was on cargo duty it was easy to slip up to the bridge where there was no guard and call the other ship with my torch. It took me a few minutes to get a reply and as soon as I did the other apprentice started changing his signalling position on the vessel. In this way it took some time for me to discover that there were not enough volunteers to get a football team to play us.

71

Disappointed, I reported the matter to the second officer and he undertook to inform the others.

I thought no more about it until a half hour later, when I was summoned to the passenger lounge where the brooding Chinese officer sat behind his desk looking at me, while the interpreter stood alongside him with a very worried look on his face. I stood there in silence while the captain was called from his sleeping bunk along with mad Robbie grinning from ear to ear. It seemed that as soon as I started signalling, a Russian tanker moored ahead of the P&O vessel had spotted me and reported the fact to the authorities.

In an almost deadly silence the interpreter asked me if I had been signalling from the bridge. I immediately owned up, and Captain Marchant nearly had a heart attack on the spot. Apprentices were his special responsibility and it appeared that the Chinese might remove me from the ship to interview me. As it was, it seemed an age as the Chinese officer thought about the matter; and I must admit I was scared. Could it be a sentence to work in a salt mine or something, I thought?

After some time the intrepreter informed me that because I had been observed it was fortunate that I had confessed; he said I was to write out a full confession in triplicate at once and this was to be signed by the captain, then my fate would be decided.

When I returned to the lounge I was sweating and trembling. The interpreter then informed me, in a very official voice, that I had violated the port rules of Shanghai and this was an extremely serious offence. However, the merciful officer had taken into account my youthful age and the lack of evidence that I might be a spy.

It was at this point, as I was recovering from the strain, that the Chinese officer suddenly spoke in perfect English: "You are a bloody fool. Don't be so silly in future." Then I was allowed to leave, and to receive a very severe rollicking from Captain Marchant in his cabin.

I certainly learnt a harsh lesson that night, and the sight of Captain Marchant's face, almost purple with rage, remained equally frightening for the rest of the voyage.

Leaving Little Bitter Lake, Suez Canal.

Moored at Calcutta.

Loading stores in Port Said.

Elephant landing in New Brunswick, Canada, the *City of Stafford*.

Loading heavy cargo on *City of Johannesburg,* Tilbury, London.

City of York leaving Beira before I joined her.
Picture taken from the *City of Johannesburg.*

City of Johannesburg, 1956.

Gibraltar harbour.

Gibraltar main street, 1959.

At Gibraltar with mates from ship.
Eric on left.

At Mrs Cooper's lodgings when attending
Devonport Technical College.

In Arabian headdress on the *City of Newport* at Basrah.

Crew on board the *City of Ottawa*.

Jill and Eric during their courtship.

City of Ottawa.

Next day, another side of the Chinese character became apparent when the interpreter announced that the authorities were very sorry that we had not had a football match, and were laying on a coach to take us to see the sights of Shanghai. Many of the crew accepted the invitation and much enjoyed the excursion.

The Chinese guide took the opportunity to show us the places where they had fought the National Chinese in the revolution some years before. He also showed us the old Shanghai racecourse now being turned into a people's park. It was depressing, though, to see what seemed to be the whole population dressed in blue trousers and padded jackets, with the only splash of colour being the odd foreigner in western dress.

Our trip ended at a sort of club like a seamen's mission, where our Indian crew were able to buy a large number of sewing machines at a very cheap price and fill every spare bit of space in the coach. Then came the invitation we could not ignore, which was to stay and see some Chinese entertainment. This proved to be a play with wonderfully dressed actors and actresses talking in very high pitched Chinese, accompanied by a man playing a one string violin. This went on for two hours and we were under orders from the ship's officers to be very polite and say we enjoyed it. The truth be told, we were all very glad to get back to the ship and familiar surroundings.

Some three days later we sailed for Sing Tao. Here we had even more soldiers guarding us and I was confined to my cabin for fear of upsetting the Chinese. It seems amazing now but at this port we loaded ore to make a metal that was a major part of the American space race with the Russians. On arrival back in the UK the ore would be transferred from our ship to an American freighter and taken to the USA.

A couple of days later we were back on our passage south, passing outside the island of Formosa to return to Hong Kong. It was at this point that the captain was discovered dead in his bunk, and we were a very shaken crew as we arrived in the port with the chief officer in command. During the day the captain's body was landed, and after a medical check a funeral was held in a church and he was buried in a local cemetery.

73

g

This sad episode resulted in only a brief visit to Hong Kong before we were on our way to Singapore. For the time being we were left on watch and thankfully left alone by mad Robbie. However, just before we arrived in Singapore he announced that the a new captain was joining us there and his ominous words to me were: "I will sort *you* out on the way home."

To hear such comments really filled me with gloom and some fear and I finally decided to do something about it. When the new captain arrived I resolved to make a complaint to him.

9

A Fresh Start

Captain John Maclaren was indeed a very different man to his predecessor. He was small in stature but interested in his crew and willing to listen to what I had to say. Luckily for me he took an instant dislike to Robbie, and he listened with some interest to my experiences over the voyage before he joined the ship. I must admit that I was near to tears as I recounted the tale. After I had finished, he said, "That's alright son, no apprentice is bullied on a ship I command. I will sort it out and you have nothing to fear."

I had no knowledge of what was said between the two senior officers, but the chief officer hardly spoke to me for the rest of the voyage. I worked together with my mate Michael and life was indeed much better. So at last, on the 25th June 1956, this nightmare voyage ended in Hull and I was able to proceed on to some home leave.

As it happened, my father and mother were in London and I travelled to meet them and we stayed at the Merchant Navy Hotel in Lancaster Gate. On his arrival my father admitted that he had visited the Ellerman Head Office in London and, as a captain, had been able to see the superintendent who had responsibility for me.

My father's opening remark was an eye opener: "Had a rough voyage, have you, Eric?"

"Too true!" I replied.

He smiled, "That's part of going to sea, my boy, but you will be glad to know the company are satisfied and have no complaints against you."

It struck me that I had received what I deserved after my actions on the *City of Stafford* before joining my present ship. However, I certainly did not admit that to my father or mother.

After a short leave at home I rejoined the *City of Johannesburg* in South Shields, where the ship was undergoing a refit. There was some good news and some not quite so good. Mad Robbie was leaving the vessel and my position on the ship was much improved. However, our next trip was back to Pakistan and India, and this was a bit of a disappointment as it was the rainy season on the subcontinent.

It was a routine trip until we approached the Red Sea in the third week of October. We were aware that the situation was not normal in the Suez Canal; Russian pilots had taken the place of the French and British Pilots, and the system of changing pilots in the Bitter Lakes was scrapped, with the one pilot taking the ship all the way to Port Said in the Mediterranean. Just the same, we were surprised to be escorted part way from Aden by a British cruiser and followed by a fast Russian freighter. We were a little concerned, for we had on board forty tons of plimsols loaded in Calcutta to be discharged in Port Said and we did not know how the Egyptians would deal with the situation.

On our passage through the canal we had one of the new pilots and he only gave orders as required, otherwise refusing to answer any of our questions. On arrival at Port Said, therefore, we pulled out of the convoy heading into the Mediterranean and moored to buoys in the harbour. It was very noticeable that our normally urbane captain was not his normal quiet self. He began shouting from the bridge as we completed the task of mooring to the buoy.

"Open the two hatches with the cargo at once," he shouted as the crew left their docking stations. Then as soon as the agent came aboard at the gangway, he was there to meet him, demanding to know when the two cargo barges with Egyptian dockers would be arriving.

We had finished our passage at midday on the 27th of October and it was four o'clock before we were ready to discharge our cargo. By this time it almost looked as though Captain Maclaren was going to have a fit.

We had been able to see plenty of troop movements along the canal and it was obvious after our arrival that there was a military presence in Port Said.

It was our job as apprentices to place large lights called clusters in the hold to give the dockers light after dark. However, like the rest of the officers, no one could satisfy our captain by doing the job quickly enough. The largest part of the cargo was in the hatch where I was stationed. As the last two or three loads were being discharged, I was standing by on deck ready to take in the clusters and store them away for our next sea passage. To my surprise, the captain suddenly appeared alongside me and told me to board a launch alongside and read the ship's draft. (This was a check to see the depth of the ship in the water below the waterline.) Now this was normally the third officer's job and I simply said I would tell him.

"No," the captain almost screamed, "you do it!"

To put it mildly, I jumped to it, and as I was climbing aboard the launch I heard the third officer shout in furious tones, questioning what I thought I was doing. As I turned to answer, the captain was ordering him to take in the clusters from the hold and to stop arguing about it.

So it was a rather shaken crew that was standing by on deck to let go the ropes for the next half hour while we awaited a pilot to guide us to sea. In fact, it was only when this pilot disappeared back into his boat that Captain Maclaren regained his cool and eventually handed the control of the ship to the second officer at midnight, then disappeared below to his cabin without another word.

It was just twenty-four hours later that we suddenly had quite a shock when a warship without lights called us up with a signal light and asked our identity, port of destination and cargo carried. At the time we were carrying over 8,000 chests of tea bound for our next port which was Tilbury, together with a large quantity of jute. On completion of the necessary information to the warship we were ordered to hold our course and speed and not to deviate to the south.

We then passed ship after ship of the British and French invasion force heading towards Egypt. It was at this time we realised that our captain had known all along of the invasion and this was the reason for his behaviour in getting the vessel to sea from Port Said as quickly as possible.

By the time we reached the Western Mediterranean on the 31st October, we could hear the reports of ships sunk at the entrance to the canal and we knew we would not be going back that way for some time.

It turned out that another older and slower Ellerman ship was ahead of us with a cargo from India, and both ships docked on the same day in the Thames, with fourteen thousand chests of tea for the tea merchants between them. They were doing a roaring trade at the time, as a cup of tea was regarded as essential to most families and everyone was buying and hoarding such items of food and drink.

10

Better Times

Once again, after a short leave, I was to rejoin the *City of Johannesburg*, bound for a three month voyage trip to South Africa. There I was to see the beauty of the Cape of Good Hope and enjoy the hospitality of many good people. However, the winds of change were coming to this area of the world and the old way of life was about to change dramatically.

Our ports of call were Cape Town, Port Elizabeth, East London and Durban in South Africa and Lourenco Marques and Beira in Potuguese Mozambique. The cargo was a rich mixture of consumer goods such as whisky, cars, lorries, luxury food and goods, clothes and even shoes. Much of this was bound for Bulawayo and Salisbury in Southern Rhodesia. (Unfortunately a very different situation exists today in that same country, now named Zimbabwe.)

One pleasant aspect of the voyages to South Africa was meeting friendly girls working in the various Flying Angel Missions on the coast. These missions offer all seafarers a hospitable place to go and can help with emergency assistance, family liaison, support and counselling.

I was now to spend a year running to South Africa from the UK and the Continent on two more ships of the Ellerman and Bucknall line. The first was the *City of York* 14,941 gross tons, and built at Vickers Armstrong shipyard in Newcastle. This magnificent vessel carried 108 passengers and cruised at 17 knots. The ship was without doubt the height of my apprenticeship, and as such, the apprentices even had their own steward, which was an unheard of luxury. All the public rooms were of the highest standard and came with a very large crew to meet the needs of the wealthy and important passengers the ship carried. It really was a very special ship in which to serve.

Voyaging in this ship was notable to me for two reasons. The first being that I had met a very attractive young lady in East London, South Africa, called Audrey and we had become very good friends. I had now been able to meet her on two further visits to the port. However, the second incident was not so pleasant. I had gone ashore in Durban, on our way northwards along the South African coast, and visited a well known ice skating rink in the city. With a certain amount of bravado in front of my mates, I tried skating, even though I had no previous experience! Of course, the inevitable happened, and I fell over with a real bump and lost consciousness. When I awoke I was being treated in an ambulance and on my way to hospital. After a restless night in a private room (the company looked after me well) I was given to understand that I could have fractured my skull and was to be kept in for a week under observation. As the *City of York* was sailing next day, I was left behind and signed off the ship.

It did not take the Cornish community in Durban long to find out where I was. I already knew Mr and Mrs Webber, who came from my home town, and soon I was having quite a few visitors. Meanwhile my father was at home on leave prior to taking command of a brand new ship, the MV *Crestbank*, then being built in Belfast. On hearing the news of my accident he immediately contacted his company superintendent in Durban. I believe the conversation went something like this:

"I have contacted you to ask a favour, sir?"

"Yes, Captain Kemp," the superintendent replied, "if I can help I will."

"My son has had an accident in Durban and has been left in hospital all alone. Will you go up and visit him, and take some fruit or reading material?"

80

"Very well, Captain. I have four ships here at the moment and am very busy, but I will see what I can do."

Unfortunately, when he arrived at my room I was surrounded by fourteen Cornishmen all talking at once and there were flowers and magazines everywhere. The superintendent quickly left, muttering to himself. He had indeed realised that the Cornish looked after their own.

In due couse the doctors decided I did not have anything wrong. Fourteen days later I was able to rejoin the *City of York*, now on the way homewards, and the end of my days as an apprentice were rapidly approaching.

After a short leave I was delighted to be promoted to the exalted rank of 4th officer, and I was to join the *City of Carlisle* in London for another voyage to South Africa. This ship was built in 1946 at the yard of Cammel Laird at Birkenhead and had a gross tonnage of 9,913 tons. There was accommodation for twelve passengers. The steam engine was geared to three turbines and had a service speed of over sixteen knots. The drawback for officers was the fact that they had to look after six hatches; hence the reason for having a 4th officer to help.

Once again I was to have the luxury of visiting East London and Durban, meeting Audrey twice more on our outward journey and seeing her whenever I was free to get ashore. I must admit I was really keen on her and was even thinking of moving to South Africa to be with her, but Audrey rejected my advances. I must in all honesty say that with hindsight I am very glad she did.

So at the end of October 1957 I was still serving on the *City of Carlisle* as we set off for South Africa once more. It turned out to be a disappointing voyage. In East London Audrey refused to see me and that left me in some despair. Then in Durban our master, Captain Williams, announced that we would not be returning home, but would be proceeding on to Chittagong, in East Pakistan, to commence loading for the East Coast of America.

This voyage turned out to be a bit of a trial. In Durban a supply of fresh water was pumped into a fuel tank, and this involved a three day delay and a lot of trouble for the engineers, as the contaminated fuel had to be removed and the tank cleaned.

Our berth was a long way from the city, giving us nowhere to go when we went ashore, and that added to the gloom of leaving the South African trade route.

On arrival in Chittagong we experienced long delays in loading as the port was only getting 20 tons of cargo a day to load for the United States. So we spent Christmas at the port and then moved on to Calcutta for the New Year. We proceeded to Vishakhapatnam, and Madras before calling at Trincomalee in Ceylon and finally leaving the subcontinent on our long voyage to Boston, New York, Philadelphia and Baltimore.

This sea passage was marked by very bad weather in the western Mediterranean, south of the Balearic Islands. One very large wave badly damaged the steel plates on the starboard side of the bow. It was then necessary to proceed to Gibraltar for repairs and these took three days. It proved a most pleasant experience, with English newspapers and strawberries on sale in the shops and even policemen looking like our own at home.

Our passage across the Atlantic was a routine one and we were soon discharging the cargo at a rapid rate and moving southwards along the American east coast. Then, at the last port of discharge, Baltimore, my indentures had expired, and I was relieved to come home to study and take my second officer's exams of competency.

I left the ship on the 14th of March 1958, having completed two years of pre sea-training on HMS *Worcester*, and three years at sea with the Ellerman and Bucknall Steamship company. By the time I left the *City of York* my wages had risen to sixteen pounds a month, and as fourth officer on the *City Of Carlisle* I had earned the magnificent sum of thirty-six pounds, twelve shillings and sixpence a month. I had saved two hundred and fifty pounds and, with the help of the dole money, I could expect to survive at school and pay the fees, as well as the travelling expenses, necessary to take the exams over the next sixteen weeks or so.

It was a wonderful journey by train to New York, calling at Philadelphia on the way, and then, as a second class passenger, I boarded the RMS *Queen Elizabeth* on my way home to Southampton, before finally catching the train to St. Ives.

11

A Certificated Officer

Now I had to prepare to study and pass my second mate's examinations. So with a collection of study books I presented myself at the Devonport Technical College (now the Plymouth University) to enrol for the course.

In some ways I was lucky. There were a number of candidates from St. Ives and, after an interview with the Principal of the Marine faculty, I teamed up with one of them. He was Tommy Stevens who was studying for his chief officer's certificate.

Fortunately I had received some leave pay and twelve weeks' study leave. Together with my own savings I now had the princely sum of approximately four hundred pounds.

My first task with Tommy was to go round to his 'digs' at lunchtime and meet his landlady. She was a small middle-aged woman called Mrs Cooper, and had a shrill voice that in no uncertain terms informed me her boarders always kept to the rules of the house. These were: no alcohol on the premises, no smoking in the bedrooms and no early morning returns from drinking parties.

The rent for bed, breakfast and evening meal was four pounds fifteen shillings per week which did not include weekends. In actual fact the lady had a cousin who had a butcher/grocer shop and with his help was able to cater at a minimum cost. Some of the meals included the smallest eggs I have ever seen. More often than not we supplemented our meagre rations by buying fish and chips after the evening meal. It was a joy to get home to mother at the weekend and have a really good feed for a couple of days.

Mrs Cooper also had a daughter of very large proportions living at home, and with a very loud voice to match. The landlady was always trying to marry her off and we avoided any commitment like the plague.

Classes were extremely intensive at the technical college, but the lecturers treated us very well and we were even allowed to smoke in class. The three months of the summer term were very agreeable, but for the first time in my life study really meant study. I only had a finite amount of money, and without a certificate my future prospects in the Merchant Navy were not at all good.

After twelve weeks we were allowed to sign on the dole and this was to prove useful to me after I sat the exams in Cardiff in July 1958. I had worked hard and to my delight I passed the written exam with some ease. However, overflowing with confidence, I was actually doing quite well in my oral exam until I managed to collide my vessel with a trawler while fishing! As a result I had to retake the oral exam. It did not help when the examiner commented that had I not made such a mistake, I would have passed with flying colours.

Due to the summer holidays I could not retake the exam until well into September.

12

Romance and an Angry Captain

It turned out to be a delightful holiday, as I had started to date a young blonde schoolteacher whom I had known since my primary schooldays, named Jillian England. Her father, Sam England, owned a garage and ran a local taxi service. During the holiday I was able to help around the business.

It was through helping at the garage that I came into close contact with the two Hayle Trinity House Pilots who kept their cars in Sam's garage, ready to respond to ships' needs at any time of day. On one particular Wednesday I was able to have a long talk with Jimmy Ninnis, one of these pilots, and was invited to come with him next morning, when he was to pilot the 800 gross tons coaster *Gardience* (owned by the Cresence Shipping Company) out of Hayle to proceed to Barry. There she was due to load coal again for the Hayle power station.

Next morning, at the early hour of 3.30am, I joined Jimmy and his co-pilot Dan Paynter to travel to Hayle. Dan was driving the car and would then come back to St. Ives, while we would disembark into the pilot cutter *Ada* to come ashore.

Before joining the ship, Jimmy visited a barge berthed near Lelant, a mile or so from the ship, to call the master who lived there. To his surprise the captain had joined the ship the day before, after a month's leave, and a very angry wife voiced her strong disapproval of being woken at that time of the night.

85

Jimmy was in no way disturbed but carried on cheerfully talking to me as we approached our destination.

As we climbed up the gangway he explained his normal procedure when piloting this vessel out to sea.

"First things first, Eric. Off to the galley to see the cook and get a mug of tea."

As things transpired it was not our first stop. The ship had all the accommodation aft, towards the stern, and forward of this were two cargo holds. The accommodation for crew was below the level of the main deck and entered by a stairway connecting to the crew's cabins, the galley and mess rooms, and the officer's saloon. Above this was another deck where the officers' and captain's cabins were situated. As we reached the first alleyway we met a very wan looking steward who was trying to clean the general area of the passageway.

"What's the matter, boy?" Jimmy said kindly.

"I'm finished in this ship," the steward replied. "I went ashore last night and got thrown out of the last pub that I was allowed to visit in Hayle, and got back to the ship early, about 9.30pm. Of course, I'd forgotten my key to the accommodation, and the door being locked, the skipper had to get up and let me in through the galley skylight. He's logging me, and I'll have to pay a fine because I didn't open the crew door aft so he was disturbed three more times last night to let the other members of the crew get to their cabins. Anyway, he seems to be in a bad mood and I'm going to join another ship when we get back to Barry."

In due course, we found three more of the crew in the same situation and it seemed a mutiny was growing before we had even left the quay. Eventually we got our mug of tea and approached the captain's cabin. He was indeed in a bad mood, but his tale of returning to the ship was a really funny story; and we had the greatest trouble in keeping straight faces as we listened while sipping our tea.

It seemed the captain had returned early the afternoon before, to allow the ship's mate to attend his daughter's wedding in Hayle. He had found the officer in his bunk sleeping off a large quantity of alcohol and was unable to wake him.

The captain's pride and joy on the ship was the wheelhouse which he looked after with a great deal of zeal. Normally the brasswork would shine to such an extent that you could see your face reflected in the gleaming metal. Now it was untended and green. The lockers and chart table bore the scruff marks and stains of spilt tea. While, horror of horrors, two tramps were sleeping peacefully on the deck in front of the ship's wheel. Naturally they were thrown out without ceremony.

On proceeding to the ship's mess room he found the luggage and two company representatives demanding explanations as to why no one was on watch and their spare cabin was locked and unprepared for passengers.

The captain himself had to get the keys and prepare the accommodation, as the steward was nowhere to be found. He then returned home with the said gentlemen to get them a meal from a very disgruntled wife.

When he returned to the ship he found that the mate had gone ashore and it was left to him to keep watch aboard. Then, during the late evening, he had to assist his crew aboard in a drunken state.

To say he was enraged would be an understatement, and his temper had not improved at this early hour as Jimmy prepared to pilot the ship to sea.

The *Gardience* only had a hand capstan at the stern to heave mooring ropes. While at the bow the chief officer had a power windlass to heave the vessel off the berth with a mooring rope connected to a post halfway across the harbour. So, as well as the lone sailor at the stern, the captain, pilot and myself had to man the handles of the capstan and heave the vessel's stern by means of another rope fastened to a second post out in the harbour. This was hard labour with the wind blowing the ship against the quay.

So, of course, all this extra work made the master even more unhappy and as the ship left the port, he could be heard all over Hayle shouting at the crew and arguing with the mate. Even after the ship had crossed the bay and Jimmy and I climbed down the pilot ladder into the pilot boat *Ada*, and started off to St. Ives harbour, he could still be heard venting his spleen on the mate who was suffering a king sized hangover at the time.

Jimmy's final remark was typical of a ship's pilot, "All in a day's work, Eric."

13

Back to Sea

By October I had a brand new second officer's certificate and joined the *City of Newport* in Liverpool as third officer. This was another of the Liberty ships built by the US during the war and had loaded over 10,000 tons of general cargo for the Persian Gulf.

The voyage proved one of the longest I had experienced at sea, due mainly to over-stowed cargo preventing its discharge at the correct ports, resulting in the ship having to call twice at two ports in the Gulf.

During this time I was taken sick in the port of Umm Said in the British protectorate of Qatar. Although it proved to be a severe chill with a high temperature, the doctors were fearful that it was polio and I was removed ashore from the ship for observation. I was to remain in hospital at the port for two very pleasant weeks in the company of some lovely British nurses, before returning to the ship at Mina al Ahmadi for further duty.

We also spent over two months in and around the Shatt al Arab river between Basrah in Iraq, and Khorramshahr and Abadan in Iran, or Persia as it was then. These were uncertain times and British officers were not popular.

In Basra, President Kassim had come to power and he was importing arms from Russia which were arriving at the port on the same jetty as our ship. A high fence and screens separated us from the Russian ship with this cargo.

The political situation meant it was very difficult for crew members to get medical treatment, and as luck would have it I developed a really bad toothache. I almost emptied the medical cabinet of codeine tablets and Captain Rigg insisted that I have treatment ashore.

I was taken to old Basrah Town where, in streets that resembled Britain in the middle ages, I was treated at a private practice. This consisted of one room divided by a large curtain, behind which the dentist and his family lived, and a surgery which had the oldest dentist's chair I had ever seen (circa nineteen hundred and five). It was far from hygienic, and my mouth became infected after I had the extraction.

Three days later I was taken to a new hospital where I joined a large number of local people, including women, to see a doctor. To say I was embarrassed was an understatement. In the waiting room, in front of many males and females in their traditional dress, I was forced to take my pants down and receive a jab with a large needle into my posterior; only to be told in the next room that my infection would last for a fortnight and there was nothing to be done but take more tablets. Eventually I got some real relief from a doctor in Abadan, down-river from Basrah, who prescribed some really powerful medicine to ease the pain.

After leaving the Shatt al Arab river we had to return to two of our former ports with over-stowed cargo; and I must say it was a real relief to get away from this area and sail to Chittagong, in East Pakistan, where we began loading jute and other cargo for Hull and Dundee.

It proved a difficult matter to find enough cargo for the ship to leave the subcontinent, and our voyage seemed like a never-ending nightmare. On our way we were to run into really bad weather approaching Malta in the Mediterranean. In an intense gale the ship slowed down and then had to heave to as hurricane winds swept breaking seas right over the decks, causing a lot of superficial damage to deck and lifeboat equipment.

During the height of this storm we witnessed an extremely unusual event, when a very large flock of huge black raven-like birds descended on the ship and occupied every space they could find to take refuge from the weather. They managed to occupy the saloon, the forepeak stores, the navigating bridge and even the captain's bathroom. They had lost all fear of humans and stayed with us for some thirty-six hours, leaving an unholy mess behind them, as you can imagine.

14

Another Run to India and North America

So it was that I returned home only to be posted to join the *City of Ottawa*, 7,662 gross tons, a twelve passenger ship that spent the time running between Canada, America and the Indian subcontinent.

I joined this ship in Gibraltar after a hair-raising first air-flight for me. The plane was an ancient Andover and it did not help my confidence when the flight attendant ordered us to fasten our seatbelts over the Spanish mountains with the remark: "You will feel the plane shudder a bit, it is getting rather old." Then the landing at Gibraltar proved most forbidding as we swooped into what seemed a very small airport.

Following a very pleasant stay of two days in Gibraltar, the *City of Ottawa* arrived and we were then on our way to India in what proved to be my last visit to that country as a ship's officer. After a routine trip around India and Pakistan we sailed once more for Canada, where I left the ship in Montreal in October 1959. We had been five months on board.

There was a week's delay, which proved to be a nice holiday for me, spent together with the Ship's Chief Steward (who seemed to have influence in high places), then we travelled home in the Curnard Liner *Saxonia*. Dudley (the chief steward) had

Eric as fourth officer on board the *City of Carlisle*, 1957.

The St. Ives branch line which always brought me home.

Fiancée Jill's front balcony looking out over Porthmeor Beach, St. Ives. Eric lived at the other end of the beach.

Eric and Jill's wedding.

Eric's parents Captain John and Mrs Ann Kemp, with Jill's mother Kate England, at the wedding of Eric and Jill.

MV Ilorin Palm.

MV Burutu Palm, 1962.

The yacht *Abredua* alongside MV *Burutu Palm*.

Abredua winched onto *Burutu Palm*.

The *Rose of Sharon*, 1963. A St. Ives fishing boat and the successor to *Sweet Promise*, the boat utilised by Eric's mother to try and dissuade him from going to sea!

persuaded the agents to book us first class, so I came home in style to sit my Chief Officer's Certificate which I obtained in April 1960 in London.

j

15

Change of Company
and Marriage

After my exam I returned home to Cornwall, and I proudly showed my pass result letter to my fiancée Jill as we travelled the five miles by road from the railway station at St. Erth to St. Ives in her father's taxi.

"Now we can fix the date to get married," I said.

"Already fixed," was the reply. "It's the 22nd of August."

"Oh," I said, "I suppose I'll have to get some relieving duties to see me through the next four months."

That proved more difficult than I imagined, as Ellerman lines seemed determined to make me serve on a vessel bound for Pakistan that was due back in the UK in August. However, I did not trust the company anyway, as they had a nasty habit of announcing to the crew abroad that the vessel they were on had new orders and was proceeding to America instead of the UK.

The only other work they could offer me, despite owning over a hundred ships, was occasional short voyages with leave without pay, which was not really acceptable to me. I did serve two weeks in the *City of Port Elizabeth,* 13,182 gross tons, before being sent home for three weeks without pay. This really annoyed me, as I had to work in my prospective father-in-law's garage selling petrol and generally helping out, just to cover the cost of my meals; and meanwhile my parents were both away at sea. So by the end of May I phoned the Ellerman personnel office and announced I would quit the company if I did not get paid work until my marriage in August.

What a mistake, I was granted an immediate position as second officer on the *City of Poona*, a sister ship of the *City of Carlisle*, then berthed in Hull discharging a cargo from India.

My first reaction on joining the ship was one of alarm. The master was Captain Worsley, a retired master brought back on temporary duty at the age of seventy-two. His sight was very poor and he was quite forgetful. The chief officer had served in the Merchant Navy during the 1939-45 war and at sixty-eight years old he was supposed to be retired as well. He was known as Stonewall Jackson and left as much work as possible to his junior officers.

After leaving Hull we proceeded to Antwerp, Rotterdam and Hamburg. On three occasions the ship was on dead slow speed with the master insisting it was foggy, when I could see light buoys over five miles away. My final humiliation came when we approached the Thames pilot station and sailed by the pilot vessel without slowing down, despite my protests that I could read pilot on the side of the cutter while the captain was insisting that it was a coaster. We finally stopped five miles further up the channel and had to wait over half an hour for the small cutter from the pilot vessel to catch us up. Naturally the captain disappeared from the bridge as the pilot arrived and I was left to face the not unprovoked anger of the poor man forced to make the long trek to us in a very small boat. In fact, by the time we arrived at Tilbury I was fed up listening to the complaints.

As luck would have it, a Merchant Navy Union representitive arrived to see us after we came alongside in the enclosed dock. I told him my troubles and he advised me to try my luck with the Palm Line, owned by Unilever, whose vessels were engaged on the West Africa trade. "They are only away for fourteen weeks," he said, "and they are building a lot of new ships. I am sure they would allow you to work around the UK while you wait to get married."

So it was with some relief that I joined a brand new vessel, the *Ilorin Palm*, in Amsterdam on the 14th of July as second officer. As it happened my parents arrived in Rotterdam the same day on board the Andrew Weir motor vessel *East Bank*, and I was able to visit them for a few hours and give them the news that I had joined the Palm Line.

From then I was employed right up until the week of my marriage at the Bedford Road Methodist Church in St. Ives. My father attended the ceremony in full uniform as was I also. It turned out a brilliant day and we had a marvellous honeymoon in Dublin for two weeks. It was the start of a wonderful lasting partnership that is still going strong as I write these lines, after fifty years.

Of course, on arrival home I found a mass of telegrams and messages ordering me to join various ships at once. Less than a week later I was at sea, bound for the west coast of Africa, starting a whole new chapter in my life and leaving my school teacher wife to manage on her own.

I was to spend five years in the Palm Line, often working under extreme conditions of heat and also serving on two vessels owned by the Nigerian National Line while Nigerians were trained to take our places.

I was to serve on most classes of ships owned by the Palm Line, where as well as being ship's officers we were expected to carry out duties as stevedores with African untrained labourers on the African coast. However, the company was generous in allowing my leave to attend the birth of my first son Ian in December 1961, and on a number of other occasions of importance they were likewise very considerate to me during the time I was with them.

The final chapter of this book will tell the story of my time spent on the MV *Burutu Palm* between June 1962 and October 1963 as second officer, to show how life was on the West African trade.

16

A Golden Ending
after an Eventful Voyage

On the 24th June 1962 I had made the long rail journey from my home in Cornwall to the South Docks in Liverpool to join the MV *Burutu Palm* as second officer. On my arrival at the quayside I found the vessel being loaded with a general cargo for Dakar, Freetown, Monrovia, Abidjan, Takoradi, Lagos, Burutu, Warri and Sapele; all ports in the Gulf of Guinea, West Africa.

In many respects this ship, *Burutu Palm*, was much superior to the last Palm Line vessel I had sailed on, the SS *Ashanti Palm*, which as a steamer was a nightmare. Built in 1947, her steam winches and main engine were continually breaking down. The accommodation was spartan in the extreme, with a notice in place by the officers' cabins, put there by a wag of the past, which read 'Skid Row'!

Just the same, I was not all that confident as I surveyed the busy scene on the quay, with cargo ranging from bags of salt, to large consignments of Guinness and whiskey in wooden crates, together with cars, lorries, furniture, tinned foods and even bales of very expensive silks and satins for the ladies of West Africa. I knew the ship did not carry apprentices and was an extremely hard working one for the three junior deck officers. On board I could expect good equipment but I would have to work even harder than usual. Indeed, here was one of the workhorses which made a real profit for the company in its West African trade. A reliable Doxford engine and electric winches helped. However, it still meant a great deal of checking valuable cargo and working long hours in the West African tropical heat.

The *Burutu Palm* had been built at Sunderland by Short Bros Ltd in 1952 and was the first ship built for the Palm Line, which had been formed from the fleet of the United Africa Company, both shipping company subsidiaries of the giant Unilever conglomerate. Her gross tonnage was 5,410 and she had a speed of twelve knots. Cargo was carried in five main cargo holds, with an additional tonnage hatch on the poop which was rarely used for official cargo. Instead the African crew members on outward voyages would use it to carry all the cheap secondhand goods they could find in ports such as Liverpool, to resell in West Africa at a handsome profit for themselves.

Soon I was on board being introduced to the other officers and the master who was Captain Swan, a small quiet gentleman and quite restrained in his manner; while the Chief Officer Mr Brand was a burly cheerful man, and the third officer was a taciturn Scotsman, whose name, along with that of the other officers, I have to admit has been forgotten with the passing of the years.

Time passed quickly with all the hard work on board and we were a happy crew. Just two and half months later we were back in Tilbury with a cargo of sawn timber, logs, groundnuts and coffee. With the voyages being quite short I was quite happy to stay on the ship for another three, which brought me to 2nd of May 1963.

On that date I joined in Tilbury to find that we were loading for the usual ports but then, instead of returning to the United Kingdom, we were bound for Italy, going back to West Africa and only then returning home. This meant that we were to be away for at least five or six months and that news was not to our liking.

Of course, we all grumbled. (It is worth mentioning here that my father had sailed for two years at a time and regarded me as a ferry-boat man!) The fact is that after averaging twelve week voyages we were not happy about the change. There were two people on board who did not mind in the least, these were the captain and chief officer who had their wives along for the trip because of the time away from home.

In those days the radio officers (all nicknamed 'sparks') on our ships were not direct employees of the company but worked for Marconi Marine and usually did not join the ship until sailing day, which happened to be about a week after the rest of the crew. By this time our grumbles had died down and we were busy preparing for the voyage.

On this occasion nobody was about when the new radio officer signed on for the voyage, and we only really met him after the ship had sailed. At the time, I was on watch as we passed Dover having dropped our pilot at that point. The radio office and adjoining cabin was just behind the bridge and the officer came into the wheelhouse to watch as the white cliffs disappeared astern and we headed down channel towards Ushant and beyond.

"Well, that's the voyage started," he said by way of conversation, "they told me I would be home in twelve weeks or so in this company because I'm getting married in August, you know."

"Oh dear," was my reply, "we're on a double header and the voyage will take at least five months. Didn't they tell you when you signed on?"

I must admit his face was a picture of misery as he left the bridge and headed to the next deck below and the captain's cabin. Some time later he passed me on his way back to the cabin without a word and I returned to doing my duties as a watch keeping officer. It was quite obvious that the interview with Captain Swan had not gone well and the least said by me the better.

At 4pm I was relieved by the chief officer, who informed me that a stowaway had been found in the forward paint store. He claimed to be a Gambian national and said he wanted to return home to Bathurst and was willing to work his passage to that port. On the captain's orders this man had been locked in the crews' hospital accommodation on the poop deck, while the captain considered what to do with him.

Before leaving the bridge I looked in on the radio officer who had a half empty bottle of whisky in his hand and was not looking well at all.

"I am not going," he kept repeating in a very slurred voice.

So, after telling my relief the situation, I retired below for an hour off before getting my evening meal an hour later.

Below the captain's deck on this ship was the officers' accommodation and from there a rather grand stairway led down to a pair of wide doors which opened into the saloon where we had our meals. These doors were kept open at meal times and in the middle of the saloon, directly in line with the stairway, was the captain's table.

Fifteen minutes after we had started the meal both the captain and chief officer, and their wives, were engaged in very pleasant conversation. On the bridge the third officer had relieved the chief for his meal and all was proceeding in a very orderly manner.

Then a staggering radio officer appeared at the top of the stairway, still repeating, "I am not going to go on this voyage."

The captain and chief officer both rose to their feet as one but 'Sparks' now staggered forward and fell headlong down the stairs, landing in a heap at Captain Swan's feet.

Fortunately the chief officer's wife was a nurse, and under her direction a number of us carried the stunned officer away up to his cabin and laid him on his bunk to sleep off the effects of the alcohol.

I presumed the mild response of the captain was dictated by the presence of two ladies: "It's been quite a lively start to the voyage, don't you think, ladies and gentlemen?"

During the evening the ship proceeded westward down-channel and by midnight we were north of the Channel Islands when my night watch commenced. All was quiet, with very little shipping around, and the first two hours on the bridge passed without incident.

Then, just after two in the morning, as I was enjoying a cup of tea and a sandwich, an awful howl of pain came from the radio officer's cabin which disrupted my watch. On investigating I found Sparks doubled up with severe pains in his abdomen and in real need of medical attention.

Following a call to Captain Swan some minutes later, the master came up from below, accompanied by the chief officer and his wife, and they went into the radio officer's cabin.

Screams followed as they tried to relieve the pain, and then Captain Swan appeared with a worried look on his face. His problem was how to get help quickly.

There were no helicopters in those days and a doctor would have to be consulted. However, our radio room was out of action. Our only form of radio communication was a rather large VHF set on the bridge, used mainly for entering and leaving harbour. It had a range, on a good day, of about thirty miles and we were unsure how many would be keeping a listening watch at that time of night.

Still, it was all we had, and on the captain's order I started to broadcast an urgent message on the distress and calling frequency of Channel 16. It started with the words Pan Pan Pan to indicate that there was an urgent call for help as there was danger to human life. (It is, in fact, the second most urgent call a ship can make, superseded only by a Mayday call when there is a threat to all on board and the ship.) The message then went on: "This is the Motor Vessel *Burutu Palm.* I am in need of urgent medical advice for an injured crew member and unable to use medium frequencies to talk to a radio shore station. Can any vessel please relay my Pan message?" I then repeated the message and continued to do so at short intervals for the next half hour.

Eventually a British coasting vessel on passage from Dublin to Le Havre answered us and was able to relay our messages, via Land's End Radio, to a port health doctor based in Plymouth. On hearing the facts of the case he asked for our ship to make for Plymouth Sound and this was agreed. Sparks had been administered morphine, and as I finished my watch the ship was heading northwards towards the requested destination.

Early that morning we anchored in Plymouth Sound and both medical staff and the police boarded the ship. As our radio officer was being transferred ashore in the pilot boat on a stretcher (he was suffering from a broken pelvis and other internal injuries), two policemen gave our stowaway a very rude awakening. We watched as he was brought out on to the deck, helped into the boat, and handcuffed. It transpired that our unwanted stowaway was indeed wanted in London for attempted murder.

Following this drama we waited a further two days for a replacement radio officer. It was most frustrating for me looking at my homeland but not being allowed ashore.

In due course, and fully manned once more, we set off south to Dakar to get some cheap fuel oil and discharge the first of our outward cargo. On our way southwards we had to dodge the massive fleets of fishermen working along our track past Mauritania before arrival at our first port of call. Then we went on, past Bathurst in the Gambia (called Banjul today) and making our way westwards to Freetown in Sierra Leone. From there we called at Monrovia in Liberia, Abidjan in the Ivory Coast, Takoradi in Ghana, followed by Lagos, Burutu, Warri and Sapele all in Nigeria. The last three ports were all in the delta where the River Benin filters through the mangrove creeks to the sea. In the final port the ship was actually tied up to tree trunks over 100 miles from the sea. Then after getting rid of the last of our cargo from Europe we commenced loading giant logs and sawn timber, working twelve hours on and twelve hours off in the steaming tropical heat. A fortnight after our arrival we sailed once more back to Lagos to load coffee and groundnuts.

From there we proceeded to Takoradi in Ghana to fill the remaining space in the holds with more sawn timber and logs. A brief stop at Dakar to refuel and then we headed along the African Atlantic Coast to Safi in Morocco, some one hundred and fifty miles south of Casablanca, to discharge one hundred tons of coffee beans.

Soon afterwards we were entering the Mediterranean through the Strait of Gibraltar to arrive in Genoa, Italy. Here some of the wives arrived to travel around the Italian coast with their husbands, but my wife Jill had a young two year old son Ian to look after and we could not afford to have the trip together.

Just the same, after the hard work in West Africa the coastal voyage was very pleasant indeed. We had some time to enjoy ourselves on shore in Genoa, Leghorn and Naples. As well as buying presents for home I was able to visit Pompeii and marvel at the ruins of an ancient civilisation.

Then it was back to West Africa with another general cargo, and then finally a cargo for home. To our surprise this consisted mostly of groundnuts and coffee and very little timber. So starting in Lagos we commenced the loading of four thousand tons of bagged cargo.

On the last day before sailing a rather splendid yacht came alongside to be loaded on to our foredeck. Called the *Abredua,* it had belonged to President Nkrumah of Ghana and had been sold to a Englishman returning to the UK. Ghana, at this time, was having a financial crisis and many Europeans were getting out but were unable to bring much of their money with them. The owner had brought her to Lagos and was on the deck of the yacht on arrival. He supervised the removal of the masts before we lifted the vessel, using the ship's heavy lift derrick, on to the foredeck and made it secure. Later he was to explain to us that by buying the yacht he could get an export licence and get some of his money back that otherwise would have remained in Ghana and would have been of no value to him.

In due course, and after stops in Takoradi, Freetown and Las Palmas, in the Canary Islands, we returned to Tilbury. All had been very routine on the voyage and we were all looking forward to some well earned leave as we entered the famous Thames lock.

To say we were surprised when both security men and police in large numbers boarded our ship in the lock would be an understatement. They all gathered round the yacht and watched over it until we were alongside. Then as soon as customs had cleared the ship, the *Abredua* was loaded onto a heavy road transporter and whisked away with a police escort towards an unknown destination.

Later we were informed that the keel contained a fortune in gold and had remained a closely guarded secret all the way home. Now it was obvious why the yacht had come to Lagos in Nigeria and not waited for us to pick it up in Takoradi (Ghana).

Thus we came to the end of an interesting voyage. But I must say I was really much more interested in getting home to Cornwall than finding out about the golden end to our trip.

Later, in the Christmas period of 1964, I was to sit my exam in London and pass out just after the holiday as a Master Mariner. It was indeed a very proud moment. I had followed in my father's footsteps and could now start to change the direction of my life to one finally based in West Cornwall.

I completed my service with the Palm Line with two voyages in MV *Ibadan Palm*, a sister ship to the *Ilorin Palm* which was the first vessel I sailed on in that company.

After a short spell of waiting and coastal service in the Blue Star Line of London, I joined the Steam Vessel Service of Trinity House. Here I eventually became the junior second officer on the Trinity House vessel *Stella*, 1,500 gross tons, based in Penzance and working right around the coast of Devon and Cornwall. . . but that's a story for another time.